Understanding And Knowing God Through Some Of Life's Hard Questions

Christopher Collier

Copyright © 2012 Christopher Collier

All rights reserved.

ISBN: 9798706458874

DEDICATION

This Book is dedicated to all the True Saints of the True and Living God (Yahweh) and his Son The Lord Jesus Christ (Yeshua). To all of his Sheep's & Lamb's all over the World.

CONTENTS

ACKNOWLEDGMENTS

Thanks to the Living God [Father, Son and Holy Spirit] for life, movement and a sound mind to know his word of wisdom to rightly divide It - putting it in print form.
Thanks to Mom Betty for all she did to raise me right. I can't begin to express my gratitude to Dawn Lanore, my beautiful life's partner for your prayers, words of encouragements and sacrifices when I was at my low points in life and when I was up days and nights typing and listening to the Holy Spirits voice which was so vital to not make any mistakes or incorrect interpretations.
Thanks to Maggie Saunders, Kenyetta Clinkscale, and Evangelist Norma Albright. You all allowed the Lord Jesus to use you to get me into the Kingdom of light from darkness – you shall never be forgotten – may the Lord reward all of you for your swift obedience to his Spirit.
Thank to Pastor Benny and Suzzane Hinn - for your faithfulness and many teachings, songs and books. Teachings on the Holy Spirit that taught me so much I would have never known had you not been obedient to produce them.
Thanks to Barbara & Aniah for your prayers and first hand Critiquing and honest advice in the early stages of this books creation. Thanks to Kindle Amazon publishing Company for being available – and having a simple format to follow to download these vital words with ease. Thanks to all pastors who I met personally – who I can't began to name – Thanks to Pastor Earl and Earnestine – Pastor Kenneth and Benetta – Pastors Frankie and Kevin Julius and Laynette – Pastor Dominic - Pastor G. Craig Lewis - The entire Barr Family – Ministers Melvin, Jimmy, Rankins, Warren and Reggie – Brother and Sister Kato. A multitude of Brothers and Sisters I've met through the years who prayed for me. Rest in peace until we meet again Bryant & Nicole Foster.
Peace be to all who are in Christ Jesus our Lord.
Share how this book blessed you on our blog: christophercollier.news

1 INTRODUCTION

This book will be totally dedicated to all those who think they know about the true and living God without doing research. To those who have created in their own minds, what they want the creator of all things to be like.

This book will be totally focused on who he is, his plans to unite all nationalities in the spirit; and what he's like. I know you have seen how God is portrayed in Hollywood movies by famous actors, and how they make him out to be. A God who interacts with his creation no matter who they are and what state of mind they're in.

But that is not our God. Actually he's the opposite of what anyone can ever imagine in a un-renewed mindset. But good news, he did say that (we his creation) can understand and know him, as it is written in Jeremiah 9:23,24, where it says: "Thus says the LORD, Let not the wise man glory in his wisdom, neither let the mighty man glory in his might, let not the rich man glory in his riches: But let him that (continue to glory) glory in this, that he understands and knows me, that I am the LORD which exercise loving-kindness, judgment, and righteousness, in the earth: for in these things I delight, says the LORD." Emphasis added.

Also it is written again: "For my thoughts are not your thoughts, neither are your ways my ways, says the LORD. For as the heavens are higher than the earth, so are my ways higher than your ways, and my thoughts than your thoughts." Isaiah 55:8,9 emphasis added.

Question, have you ever searched the Holy Scriptures; and just drew a blank in the area of knowing and understanding your Creator? Well then keep reading this book, and I guarantee when you're finished, you'll have more understanding than when you first began.

The reason I said, "your Creator:" is because, he's the only one who boldly proclaimed that he made you and me, Heaven, the Universe, the Earth and everything that is in it.

He even proclaimed that he's in every person alive. If he wasn't, scripture says that everything would immediately dry up and wither away, for it is written in Job 34:14,15.

"If he (Yahweh) set his heart upon man, if he gather unto himself his spirit and his breath; all flesh shall perish together, and man shall turn again unto dust.

Scripture state also that we're all running out of time, before he removes that part of himself that keeps us all (alive naturally and spiritually) sane or saintly to a degree. For it is written again in Jeremiah 13:15,16, where it says: "Hear you, and give ear; be not proud: for the LORD has spoken. Give glory to the LORD your God, before he cause darkness, and before your feet stumble upon the dark mountains, and, while you look for light, he turn it into the shadow of death, and make it gross darkness."

And in John 12:35 it says: "Then Jesus said unto them, Yet a little while is the light with you. Walk while you have the light, unless darkness come upon you: for he that (continues to walk) in darkness knows not where he is going." Emphasis added.

Yes, Jesus is that light that's in every person born into this world, for it is written: "He (John the Baptist) was not that Light, but was sent to bear witness of that Light. That was the true Light, which continues to light every man that continues to come into the world." That's why the Holy Bible says: "The spirit of man is the candle of the Lord, searching all the inward parts of the belly." That's also why the Holy Bible tells us: "Fret not yourself because of evil men, neither be you envious at the wicked; For there shall be no reward to the evil man; the candle of the wicked shall be put out." And also "Whosoever continues to curse his father or his mother, his lamp shall be put out in obscure darkness.

John 1:8-9 / Proverbs 20:27 / Proverbs 24:19-20 / Proverbs 20:20
Emphasis Added.

Did you all know this? Isn't this amazing, that these things are recorded so we can get to know our God? It's amazing to know that he's in every man that was birthed into this world. Yes the scriptures can't lie, the only thing now is to seek the light while we have the light as Jesus (The word of God) already told us.

Maybe you're someone who knew him: (thought you knew him), or never knew him. Maybe you are someone in the valley of decision, or were someone who was serving the Lord. Until something tragic happened in your life, and you blamed God, then gave up on him; being offended. Apart from these categories of people; I've been made aware that, all other individuals just simply detest everything about the creator, meaning: (what he stands for), wanting him to leave them alone). Some are just simply Anti God and Anti

Christ. For it is written, they are: "Slanderers, hateful to and hating God, full of insolence, arrogance, [and] boasting; inventors of new forms of evil, disobedient and undutiful to parents." Emphasis added.

As a warning, this book is not a cute, (say what I want to hear) type of book). It will reveal scriptures telling the uncompromising hardcore truth; (So help me God) type of Book.

As I was studying the word of God, I came across a scripture that proved to me: we as mortal man, can indeed understand and know our creator; seeing he said we could. The question is, do we want to?

2 THIS BOOKS INSPIRATION

Jeremiah 9:23,24 inspired this book, for our God says we can: "understand and know him, that he is the LORD which exercise loving-kindness, judgment, and righteousness, in the earth: for in these things he delights in." Also I received a Heavenly vision that revealed to me that our God is love.

Before I tell you about it, isn't it a remarkable statement that he is "love." Meaning he is the source.
For it is written in 1 John 4:8 NKJV
"He who does not love does not know God, for God is love." Isn't that amazing how the Bible shows us key things about our God such as this?

It's not that he has love, he is love the source. He proved this to me in a physical open vision he gave me back in the year 2000 or 2003. I remember driving my small Chevy pickup truck on the icy roads in the State of Michigan. It was a late dark night, very little traffic was on the roads, I remember that year we had freezing rain that froze up all the roads, and the salt trucks had not had time to run yet.

I remember driving at a slow rate of speed to make it home, my house was on a steep declined street, with cars parked on one side of the road. I remember Creeping downhill very slow to reach my driveway. When all of a sudden my entire truck began to slide to the left to hit the parked cars. Nothing could stop me, I was sliding too fast towards the cars, I then lifted up my voice to God saying, Oh Lord please help me! Don't let me hit these cars! I give you praise!

I just started praising the Lord, trusting he would help me. When all of a sudden my vehicle stopped; and not only did it stop, it started moving away from the parked cars to the right, it was a miracle. The Good Lord had surely rewarded my faith in him, seeing I was moved away from the parked cars to continue downhill to my driveway. I then started to move slowly again to turn into my driveway when all of a sudden the same thing happened all over again. But at this time my faith was lifted, as I praised the Lord again, while asking him to stop my truck from hitting the parked cars like before.

He did it again, he stopped my truck on the sheet of ice and move me away from the cars again; I was so greatful to him. I was then able to turn into my driveway and Park safely without any damages to my vehicle or the others. As I sat there in my truck with the engine off, I began to thank the Lord again and praise him for sparing me, for it was notable that it was him that guided me to safety.

After I was done praising the Lord I sat there in silence with my eyes opened, when all of a sudden, it was as if a invisible door had opened in front of me; outside of the truck. It was cracked opened, but coming out from that cracked door, was an overwhelming feeling of love. Not a small feeling of love, but a love that I can only describe as being nuclear. (for lack of better words), That's the best way I could describe it. It was the feeling of love, But in an atomic measure.

That's the best way I can describe it. I can remember being frozen (unable to move) under this overwhelming grip that it had on me. The only thing I could do at this point is, roll a tear out of one eye, and say to him. "Why do you love us all like that?" Next the cracked door closed, all I could think on was; if he had swung that door wide opened, it would have literally killed me, it was that powerful.

This testimony is very much true and I was able to record it (the best way I could) with the Lord's help. After I had that experience, it left an everlasting impression upon my soul to we're no devil in hell can ever lie to me anymore, telling me that God doesn't love me (or us). For now I know that he loves us in ways we can't even imagine.

For it is written in Ephesians 3:19 NKJV, that his love "passes knowledge" and also his word tells us, "Who shall separate us from the love of Christ? Shall tribulation, or distress, or persecution, or famine, or nakedness, or peril, or sword? As it is written: "For Your sake we are killed all day long; We are accounted as sheep for the slaughter." Yet in all these things we are more than conquerors through Him who loved us. For I am persuaded that neither death nor life, nor angels nor principalities nor powers, nor things present nor things to come, nor height nor depth, nor any other created thing, shall be able to separate us from the love of God which is in Christ Jesus our Lord."
Romans 8:35-39 Emphasis Added.

3 GOD'S LOVING-KINDNESS

This next scripture will show how he started his execution of sending his loving-kindness to all humanity.

LOVING-KINDNESS
(As defined in the Old Testament)

If you will diligently give ear to the voice of the Lord your God, and will do that which is right in his sight and keep all his statutes, I will put none of these diseases upon you, which I have brought upon the Egyptians: for I am the Lord that heals you.

And the LORD passed by before (Moses) and proclaimed, The LORD, The LORD God, merciful and gracious, longsuffering, and abundant in goodness and truth, Keeping mercy for thousands, forgiving iniquity and transgression and sin, and that will by no means clear the guilty; visiting the iniquity of the fathers upon the children, and upon the children's children, unto the third and to the fourth generation.

Then after the Children of Israel heard the powerful voice of the living God speaking his commandments, they had this to say. "For who is there of all flesh, that has heard the voice of the living God speaking out of the midst of the fire, as we have, and lived? Go you near (Moses), and hear all that the LORD our God shall say: and speak you unto us all that the LORD our God shall speak unto you; and we will hear it, and do it."
Exodus 15: 26 / 34:6, 7 / Deuteronomy 5:26-27 emphasis added.

LOVINGKINDNESS
(As defined in the New Testament)

For if that first covenant had been faultless, then should no place have been sought for the second. For finding fault with them, he says, Behold, the days come, says the Lord, when I will make a new covenant with the house of Israel and with the house of Judah: Jeremiah 31:31

Not according to the covenant that I made with their fathers in the day when I took them by the hand to lead them out of the land of Egypt; because they continued not in my covenant, and I regarded them not, says the Lord. For this is the covenant that I will make with the house of Israel after those days, says the Lord;

I will put my laws into their mind, and write them in their hearts: and I will be to them a God, and they shall be to me a people: And they shall not teach every man his neighbor, and every man his brother, saying, Know the Lord: for all shall know me, from the least to the greatest. For I will be merciful to their unrighteousness, and their sins and their iniquities will I remember no more. Hebrews 8:7-9

Read all of: (Jeremiah 31:31-37)

The LORD has appeared of old unto me, saying, Yea, I have loved you with an everlasting love: therefore with loving-kindness have I drawn you. Jeremiah 31:3

The reason he could say this to Jeremiah is because, he stated also to him: "Before I formed you in the belly I knew you; and before you came forth out of the womb I sanctified you, and I ordained you a Prophet unto the nations." See Jeremiah 1:5.

Isn't that amazing that Jeremiah was in existence before he was seen by anyone in the earth? This scripture has always stuck with me, that if God knew him, he also knew of all of us before we were born. And as he knew and drew Jeremiah; to himself - God will also draw us to himself with loving-kindness also.

This next scripture will show how he planned to draw all unto himself, as he did Jeremiah.

For It is written: He (Christ Jesus) was taken from prison and from judgment: and who shall declare his generation? For he was cut off out of the land of the living: for the transgression of my people was he stricken. And he made his grave with the wicked and with the rich in his death; because he had done no violence, neither was any deceit in his mouth.

Yet it pleased the Lord (Yahweh) to bruise him; he has put him to grief: when you shall make his soul an offering for sin, he shall see his seed, he shall prolong his days, and the pleasure of the LORD shall prosper in his hand. He shall see of the travail of his soul, and shall be satisfied: by his knowledge shall my righteous servant justify many; for he shall bear their iniquities.

Therefore will I divide him a portion with the great, and he shall divide the spoil with the strong; because he has poured out his soul unto death: and he was numbered with the transgressors; and he bare the sin of many, and made intercession for the transgressors.

Isaiah 53:8-12 emphasis added.

It is written again: O continue your loving-kindness unto them that know you; and your righteousness to the upright in heart. Psalms 36:10 emphasis added.

NOTE: From the following Scriptures that the Lord has given me by revelation and rightly dividing the scriptures according to his leading. It's plain that the Lord God remembered his plan of redemption which he put in his Son from the beginning. For Revelation 13:8 says: "the book of life of the lamb slain from the foundation of the world."

Also, in Genesis 3:15 – It was foretold to the devil and Satan; that of the woman's seed (which is Christ); that his (foots) heel would bruise Satan's head.

Psalms 36:10 was inspired by the Holy Spirit to the Psalmist – when he says "continue your loving-kindness unto them that know you." Proof, did not the Lord tell all the workers of lawlessness "I never knew you" in the final judgment?

So let us remember and always keep in mind what the Lord says from the beginning: and that is.

"Glory in this, that you understand and know me, that I am the LORD which exercise (perform) loving-kindness, judgment, and righteousness, in the earth: for in these things I delight, says the LORD."

This is a word from the Lord that will stand forever, for all people throughout their generations upon Earth. This word is carried out by his Holy Spirit moving in all the Earth.

And remember how (Jesus) said to (his disciples, and us today). "My sheep hear my voice, and I know them, and they follow me." And " I am the good shepherd, and know my sheep, and am known of mine."

For God (The Father) so loved the world, that he gave his only begotten Son, (Jesus) - that whoever believes in him should not perish, but have everlasting life. For God sent not his Son into the world to condemn the world; but that the world through him might be saved. John10:14, 27 – John 3:16,17 emphasis added.

Jesus is still saying: "Therefore (this is why) my Father loves me, because I lay down my life, that I might take it again. John 10:17 emphasis added.

THE LORD JESUS CHRIST IS THE LOVING-KINDNESS OF OUR LOVING HEAVENLY FATHER TO HIS CREATION – MAY WE ALL ENTER INTO HIS GREAT GRACE, WHILE WE HAVE TIME.

For it states, "And when he (The Holy Spirit) is come, he will reprove (convict, convince) the world of sin, and of righteousness, and of judgment: Of sin, because they believe not on me (Jesus); Of righteousness, because I go to my Father, and you see me no more; Of judgment, because the prince of this; world; (the devil and Satan) is judged. John 16:8-11 emphasis added.

Notice how the New Testament scripture didn't mention how the Holy Spirit would convince the world of the Fathers "loving-kindness." Because (Jesus) the one speaking this; is the Fathers Loving-kindness and Righteousness sent into the Earth.

This he demonstrated through many eye witness accounts, Jesus says: "no man can come to me except the Father which has sent me draw him: and I will raise him up at the last day." John 6:44 (Emphasis added).

This clearly shows that those who's eyes are opened concerning who Jesus really is; are chosen of the Heavenly Father; who knows all things. On this revealing knowing, Jesus said: "he will build his Church," as stated in Matthew 16:18.

David the king said (by his Spirit) in Psalm 63:3 "Because your loving-kindness is better than life, my lips shall praise you." And in Psalm 36:9,10 "For with you is the fountain of life: in your light shall we see light. O continue your loving-kindness unto them that know you; and your righteousness to the upright in heart. So I advise you all Saints to, get to know him and be upright in your hearts. See how it says, "continue your loving-kindness unto them that know you? Sound familiar?

Remember how he said get to know him in Jeremiah 9:23,24? Plus in 2 Thessalonians 1:8 God revealed that: "In flaming fire (he will be) taking vengeance on them that know not God, and that don't obey the gospel of our Lord Jesus Christ. In seeing this, I believe we all should love him and seek him now (more than ever) to understand and know him, before time runs out. For it is written: "But if any man love God, the same is known of him."

1 Corinthians 8:3 Emphasis Added.

4 JUDGMENT EXPLAINED

Jesus' arrival brought about the coming Eternal judgment upon all of mankind; seeing we are all eternal beings; that came out of an Eternal source. The Judgment he spoke of is this: That light has come into the world and men loved the darkness rather than the light."

But, for those who want out of this darkness, this remedy was written for you. "For God (The Heavenly Father) so loved the world, that he gave his only begotten Son, (his loving-kindness, righteousness, his light); that whosoever "continues to believe" in him should not perish, but have everlasting life." Emphasis on "believe in him."

But on the flip side of this, this is written as well to all law breakers. "Truly, these times of ignorance God overlooked, but now commands all men everywhere to repent, because He has appointed a day on which He will judge the world in righteousness by the Man whom He has ordained. He has given assurance of this to all by raising Him from the dead." And also. "But for those who are self-seeking and self-willed and disobedient to the Truth but responsive to wickedness, there will be indignation and wrath. [And] there will be tribulation and anguish and calamity and constraint for every soul of man who [habitually] does evil, the Jew first and also the Greek (Gentile). Lastly, "And as it is appointed unto men once to die, but after this the judgment, and this is the condemnation, that light is come into the world, and men loved darkness rather than light, because their deeds were evil- or better yet -They love doing evil. Acts 17:30-31 NKJV
Romans 2:8-9 AMP Hebrews 9:27 Kjv emphasis added.

I have come to understand these scriptures to be true in my own life with more and more clarity. seeing I too was blinded at one time being caught up in fleshly desires and demonic influence. I had no knowledge of the light of God (which is his nature). I had no idea that I loved darkness; and that Sin was my master I was serving, until I was born again and started studying Gods word to renew my mind.

I found out also through studying this scripture, that: we're to be found in Christ Jesus, not having (our) own righteousness, which is of the law, but that which is through the faith of Christ, the righteousness which is of God by faith. (Emphasis added) John 3: 16, 19 / Philippians 3: 9

Yes, as it is written: no one can please God or do enough to earn his approval, only the Son. For it is written: "Think not that I (Jesus) am come to destroy the law, or the prophets: I am not come to destroy, but to fulfil." And then, "Jesus answered and said unto them, This is the work of God, that you believe on him whom he has sent." Matthew 5:17 / John 6:29. Emphasis added.

The Heavenly Father sent the Son to be a pattern for all mankind to see and hear about and hopefully follow his example (having his Spirit in us, enabling us). Yes, only in this are we covered in the eyes of God (the Heavenly Father).

Salvation is made simple now, we only need to believe and confess Jesus for who he truly is. As it is written: "And for their sakes (My disciples) I (Jesus) sanctify myself, that they also might be sanctified through the truth. Neither pray I for these alone, but for them also which shall believe on me through their word; That they all may be one; as you, Father, are in me, and I in you, that they also may be one in us: that the world may believe that you have sent me." For it is written: "For by your words you shall be justified, and by your words you shall be condemned.
John 17:19-21 / Matthew 12:37
emphasis added.

Though many don't agree to this, it doesn't matter. God came up with this plan of redemption; either we take it or leave it, it's our choice. Our God will not just keep silent before he make his move to close out this present world system.

Apparently if you didn't know we're all on a ticking time clock; according to the book of Daniel.

For it is written: In the latter times; (or the end times) "when the transgressors are come to the full," (emphasis added).
Also look at an account in Matthew's gospel: where a fallen Angel said to Christ: "Are you come here to torment us before the time?" (Emphasis added).

See how it says: "when the transgressors are come to the full" - And "before the time?" This is no doubt a time the Heavenly Father knows about; before he closes out this sinful world with fire and fervent heat. See: Daniel 8:23 Matthew 8:29 and 2 Peter 3:10,12.

This book will also be dedicated to a few random questions different individuals asked me about the Creator; related to his quote of us "knowing him" (the Lord), and how he "delights in executing: loving-kindness, Judgment and Righteousness in the Earth".

As for executing judgment; we're told that "the wages (charges or payment) of sin is death; but the gift of God is eternal life through Jesus Christ our Lord."

Psalm 91:7,8 shows how and why,
"a thousand shall fall at your side, (the ones who made God their habitation), and ten thousand at your right hand; but it shall not come near you. Only with your eyes shall you behold and see the reward of the wicked.

Also scripture says: "For we know him that has said, vengeance belongs unto me, I will recompense, says the Lord. And again, the Lord shall judge his people."
Romans 6:23 / Hebrews 10:30 Emphasis added.

5 HARD QUESTIONS

I believe I was shown most of these answers by God, by what I went through in my same questioning process; I just simply asked different people: if you could ask God a question, what would it be? These are some of the answers I got.

1. If this God you Christians serve is so good and is of love; why would he allow such evil to continue in the world?

2. When the devil sinned against God, why didn't God just get rid of him, instead of letting him continue to live on?

3. Why would God send people to hell to burn for Eternity?

4. Why such a harsh judgment on fallen souls?

5. What is it God wants from me?

6. Why so many rules?

7. Why can't I just live like I want to and still be accepted by God?

8. Why didn't God protect my child from dying: while I was serving him?

9. Why do bad things happen to "good people?"

10. What's the meaning of life?

11. What does God want me to do?

12. Why doesn't God answer my prayers?

13. Why does the bible say so many in the Church will not make heaven?

14. If God is our Heavenly Father; who then is our Mother?

I know for certain the Lord put it on my heart to record these questions then in turn go and search these things out in accordance to his written word, and things he'll reveal to me.

I also based this book off of questions that I myself have asked God which (in the past) did not seem to get answered but until now.

Our God obviously wants us to understand and know him, seeing he put a lot of answers in the Holy Bible and also revealed things by his Spirit to inquisitive seekers, analytical believers. I believe I was shown answers to some of these hard questions during my conversion.

I wondered, why wouldn't we as God's creation not ask him questions, who's called our near heavenly Father? Why wouldn't he answer us if we are said to be in relationship with him?

We definitely shouldn't put off these things seeing a lot of so called believers have departed from the faith – not wanting to have anything to do with the Church of Christ, the pillar and ground of the truth, giving up, to later become slanderers of what they once tried to join themselves to.

If you're one of them stay tuned to get answers from a different perspective.

6 THERE ARE ANSWERS

Jesus still says to us as believers:

"These things have I spoken to you, that you should not be offended: They shall put you out of the synagogues: (or the Churches) - yes, the time comes, that whoever kills you will think that he does God service. And these things will they do to you, because they have not known the Father, nor me."

See how this scripture shows that God puts answers in his word (which is Jesus) he's still talking to all of us in the Holy Bible to keep us from being offended and walking away. See how Jesus tells us that the information he's speaking in scripture, is so that we won't be offended? If we didn't know what was going on in this world we would indeed be offended and not have faith or hope in anything positive to come.

For what else in this world would make sense anyway? The ones who don't know the Father nor Jesus will do wrong and hate the ones that do have enlightenment and or an understanding. For it is written: If you were of the world, the world would love his own: but because you are not of the world, but I have chosen you out of the world, therefore the world continues to hate you. John 15:19 emphasis added.

Jesus also tells us plainly he's from another place; a place we are yet to see. He also wants all who come to him to allow him to convert and heal them, so you can hear his word, understand it, and keep it. He also wants us all to know that: "you are from beneath; I am from above: you are of this world; I am not of this world." John 16: 1-3 / John 8:23 Emphasis Added.

The reason he said we're from beneath is because, scripture says in (1 Corinthians 15: 47-49) that we're of an earthly nature only, earthy. Not of the heavenly nature as he is.

He said this because- he was created in the womb of Mary by the Holy Spirits creative power: and not by a seed of a man. See: Luke 1:35.

He told us this so that we would want to join him and the Father and the Spirit in Eternity.

The way he will bring us in to be with and like him and the Father; is by; "changing or quickening" us. This means to make us alive again as stated in 1 Corinthians 15:45

For it is written: "But when the kindness and the love of God our Savior toward man appeared, not by works of righteousness which we have done, but according to His mercy He saved us, through the washing of regeneration and renewing of the Holy Spirit, whom He poured out on us abundantly through Jesus Christ our Savior." And "He shall change our vile body, that it may be fashioned like unto his glorious body, according to the working whereby he is able even to subdue (or arrange) all things unto himself."

Isn't this amazing? That we as mortal man was given an invitation to be changed and live forever? Titus 3:4-6 NKJV / Philippians 3:21 Emphasis Added.

Some believe that this new life in Christ is too hard, but I say, yes it will be. if we're not yielding to his Spirit, and doing the things he says to do, yes it will be. It's truly worth it to go through whatever we have to, giving up this momentary filth for something more pure, wholesome, and grand outside of this feeble existence.

Then the questions came to me, and some asked me:

If this God you Christians serve is so good and of love – why would he allow such evil to continue in the world?

When the devil sinned against God – why didn't God just get rid of him instead of letting him continue to live on?

I pray these scriptures give an understanding to you as it did for me.
For it is written: "The heaven, even the heavens, are the LORD'S: but, the earth has he given to the children of men." Psalms 115:16

Allow yourself to see now if you will, Heaven as Gods house; and the Earth, as our house. When Satan came down into our house, he stole it by trickery from the first Man and Woman; (The Adams). This caused him to now rule and govern mankind through harsh bondage.

For it is written: the devil (called Satan), taking (Jesus) up into a high mountain, and showed to him all the kingdoms of the world in a moment of time. And the devil said to (Jesus), all this (Authority) will I give you, and the glory of them: for that is delivered to me; and to whomsoever I will I give it. If you therefore will worship me, all shall be yours. Luke 4:5-7 emphasis added.

The earth's kingdoms were delivered unto Satan through trickery: after

God had blessed (The Adams), and God said unto them, "be fruitful, and multiply, and Replenish the earth, and subdue it: and have dominion over the fish of the sea, and over the fowl of the air, and over every living thing that moves upon the earth." Genesis 1:28 emphasis added.

But instead of this happening; the LORD God ended up saying to the woman, "what is this that you have done?" And the woman said, the serpent beguiled (or tricked) me, and I did eat (of the forbidden tree). Genesis 3:13 emphasis added.

See how that all went down? That was of old, we couldn't change this, but the Heavenly Father by Christ Jesus did. For it is written:
"Now is the judgment of this world: now shall the prince of this world (The devil and Satan) be cast out." John 12:31 Emphasis added.

This was seen in a vision in Daniel 7:13-14, which says, "I (Daniel) saw in the night visions, and, behold, one like the Son of man came with the clouds of heaven, and came to the Ancient of days, and they brought him near before him. And there was given him dominion, and glory, and a kingdom, that all people, nations, and languages, should serve him: his dominion is an everlasting dominion, which shall not pass away, and his kingdom that which shall not be destroyed.

Daniel went on to reveal this. "And in the days of these kings shall the God of heaven set up a kingdom, which shall never be destroyed: and the kingdom shall not be left to other people, but it shall break in pieces and consume all these kingdoms, and it shall stand for ever. Daniel 2:44 Emphasis added.

Lastly, to seal this as utmost truth, Jesus said to his disciples. "Verily I say unto you, That you which have followed me, in the regeneration when the Son of man shall sit in the throne of his glory, you also shall sit upon twelve thrones, judging the twelve tribes of Israel." Matthew 19:28 emphasis added.

See how that all went down? Satan was dethroned and cast down, but we the Bride of Christ, have to stand guard seeing what happened to the first Eve.

The new spiritual woman (the Church) was told this by the Holy Spirit through Paul: "But I fear, unless by any means, as the serpent beguiled (or tricked) Eve through his subtlety, so your minds should be corrupted from the simplicity that is in Christ. 2 Corinthians 11:3 emphasis added.

That was then, this is now. let us be reminded by this and take heed while reading or listening to this book. Stay on guard Saints, watching out for this deceiver, so you to will stay in the simplicity of Christ, to finish well, for we are truly in troublesome times as the Bible predicted.

It is written again: "and Adam was not deceived, but the woman being deceived was in the transgression."

So now in Christ Jesus (the last Adam) – who wasn't deceived; we as the new woman (his Church, his bride), have to make sure we're not deceived also as that earthy Eve was. 1 Timothy 2:14 Emphasis Added.

The Holy Spirit warned us that Satan would use this simplicity we have in Christ as means to overthrow the last Adams wife for a reason.
No doubt, some of you who's hearing this book are well aware of the devils devices. So my advice would be to warn others, not to change, even as our God and the Lord Jesus doesn't change. Keep your eyes on all these signs of our times, so you too will know what's going on and not be caught sleeping being unaware.

To answer that last question - the first man and woman allowed such evil to (take over or continue) not God. Seeing he told Adam and Eve to have dominion over all things, and subdue all things, but they failed. But thanks be to our God, who has won us the victory. For it is written again: "But this man (The Man Christ Jesus), after he had offered one sacrifice for sins for ever, sat down on the right hand of God; From henceforth expecting till his enemies be made his footstool.

But one said to me: "ok that's understandable, but what about before Adam & Eve was put on the Earth, why didn't God just do away with (Satan) when he first sinned, instead of just casting him and his angels out of heaven into the earth?

I can't find this in Scripture – but I know the Lord personally revealed to me that that – he didn't cause this evil but he'll use it; because of the free will he gave to Man and Angelic beings. He will never control or possess us without our consent, that's just not in his nature. Even throughout Eternity, he will never do that, the only thing he did show in his word was that, he'll put things in place to deter us from changing our minds, but never will he take away the free will choice he gave to us his offspring's. Read Isaiah 66:23,24 to see proof of why I said this.

That's why Satan is now called "the Tempter" in Matthew 4:3 and 1

Thessalonians 3:5). We're currently told to resist him in James 4:7.

Scripture even shows in Revelation 20: 7, 8 how Satan is used to deceive the nations. For it is written: And when the thousand years are expired, Satan shall be loosed out of his prison, and shall go out to deceive the nations, (emphasis added).

Yes, this deceiver and tempter is used to sift mankind - to deter mankind from the faith we so desperately cling to. This will no doubt prove who we are in heart; do we won't the light or darkness; the truth or a lie, our own will or God's will.

It is written: Blessed is the man that endure (or outlast) temptation: for when he is tried, he shall receive the crown of life, which the Lord has promised to them that love him. And "Blessed are the dead that die in the Lord from henceforth: yes, says the Spirit, that they may rest from their labors; and their works do follow them." (Emphasis on: "die in the Lord") James 1:12 / Revelation 14:13 emphasis added.

And God said: Instead of erasing that problem - he used this Fallen Angelic Spirit as a tempter to temp mankind, only if mankind would start to lust after evil things in this world.

Jesus had this to say about Satan:

"You (Jews) you are of your father the devil, and the lusts of your father you will do. He was a murderer from the beginning, and didn't stay in the truth, because there is no truth in him. When he speaks a lie, he speaks of his own: for he is a liar, and the father of it." John 8:44, emphasis added.

Note: If you notice Satan is called a "father," this is what Satan wanted. Look at what the Bible records him saying within himself. "How are you fallen from heaven, O Lucifer, son of the morning? How are you cut down to the ground, which did weaken the nations? For you have said in your heart, I will ascend into heaven, I will exalt my throne above the stars of God: I will sit also upon the mount of the congregation, in the sides of the north: I will ascend above the heights of the clouds; I will be like the most High." Isaiah 14:12-14 Emphasis Added.

Here Satan was thinking about doing this, to be like the Heavenly Father (The Blessed one), not the Lord Jesus. For the "Most High" is indeed Yahweh, the "Ancient of Days." I believe when Yahweh heard his evil thoughts, he backhanded him, (and all who was looking up to him), out of

Heaven with a mighty blow. For the Lord Jesus said, "I beheld (saw) Satan as lightning fall from heaven." See how he said he saw this happen, and how fast it was?

It is also written, "And the angels which kept not their first estate, but left their own habitation, he has reserved in everlasting chains under darkness unto the judgment of the great day. For if God spared not the angels that sinned, but cast them down to hell, and delivered them into chains of darkness, to be reserved unto judgment. Lastly, "for if God spared not the natural branches (Israel), take heed unless he also spare not you." Luke 10:18 / Jude 1:6 / 2 Peter 2:4 / Romans 11:21 emphasis added.

Everything was written to paint a picture of what took place to show us what caused all of this evil in the world, and how our God doesn't mess around. Satan is now setup as our opponent to see who he can overthrow and steal from our God. He's trying to win as many Souls as he can before he's finally disposed of in the Lake of fire.

With all eyes off of Satan, the Father says it's our turn now. Saints it's our turn now, that was then, this is now. Choose to seek and walk in the light to avoid God's judgment. It's simple to understand, not hard. Jesus put it this way: This is the condemnation, that light is come into the world, and men loved darkness rather than light, because their deeds were evil. (or they just simply like doing evil) John 3:19.

For it is written again: "I (The Lord) call heaven and earth to record this day against you, (meaning mankind), that I have set before you life and death, blessing and cursing: therefore choose life, that both you and your seed may live": Deuteronomy 30:19. Emphasis added.

Please let these scriptures serve as proof- that we all have to make a choice whether we want to be like our God or like Satan and fall like him and his followers. Once I was asked a question, and that question was this. Is one night or moment with the devil worth a whole lot? So I ask you, Is a whole lot God has for you, worth momentary pleasure and fleeting pleasure(s)?

7 PROPHECY OF BEING BLINDED & SCATTERED

"And I (Yahweh) will persecute them with the sword, with the famine, and with the pestilence, and will deliver them to be removed to all the kingdoms of the earth, to be a curse, and an astonishment, and an hissing, and a reproach, among all the nations whither I have driven them: Because they have not hearkened to my words, says the LORD, which I sent unto them by my servants the prophets, rising up early and sending them; but you would not hear, says the LORD." Jeremiah 29:18,19 emphasis added.

"Therefore I (Jesus) say to you, the kingdom of God shall be taken from you, (The Hebrew Nation) and given to a nation bringing forth the fruits of it." Matthew 21:43 emphasis added.

"And when he (Jesus) was come near, he beheld the city, and wept over it, Saying, If you had known, even you, at least in this your day, the things which belong to thy peace! But now they are hid from your eyes. For the days shall come upon you, that your enemies shall cast a trench about you, and compass you round, and keep you in on every side, and shall lay you even with the ground, and your children within you; and they shall not leave in you one stone upon another; because you knew not the time of your visitation." Luke 19:41-44 emphasis added.

"And when you shall see Jerusalem compassed with armies, then know that the desolation thereof is near. Then let them which are in Judea flee to the mountains; and let them which are in the midst of it depart out; and let not them that are in the countries enter into there. For these be the days of vengeance, that all things which are written may be fulfilled. But woe to them that are with child, and to them that give suck, in those days! For there shall be great distress in the land, and wrath upon this people. And they shall fall by the edge of the sword, and shall be led away captive into all nations: and Jerusalem shall be trodden down of the Gentiles, until the times of the Gentiles be fulfilled." Luke 21:20-24 emphasis added.

"You (The Hebrew Nation) are the children of the prophets, and of the covenant which God made with our fathers, saying to Abraham, and in your seed shall all the kindred's of the earth be blessed. To you (Hebrews) first God, having raised up his Son Jesus, sent him to bless you, in turning away every one of you from his iniquities." Acts 3:25, 26 emphasis added.

Note: These Scriptures are a clear picture of what Yahweh expected of the Hebrew Nation. To take his gospel of the kingdom and bless all Nations, after first being partakers of his new will and testament. But as Jeremiah said: "But they obeyed not, neither inclined their ears, but made their neck stiff, that they might not hear, nor receive instruction."

Jeremiah 17:23 Emphasis added.

8 A STIFF NECK PEOPLE

And Moses said of old: "I know your rebellion, and your stiff neck: behold, while I am yet alive with you this day, you have been rebellious against the Lord; and how much more after my death?" Deuteronomy 31:27 emphasis added.

Then Jesus said anew: "O Jerusalem, Jerusalem, you that kill the Prophets, and stone them which are sent unto you, how often would I have gathered your children together, even as a hen (continues to gather) her chicks under her wings, and you would not." Matthew 23:37 Emphasis Added.

Then Paul said: "Take heed therefore unto yourselves, and to all the flock, over the which the Holy Ghost has made you overseers, to feed the church of God, which he has purchased with his own blood. For I know this, that after my departing shall grievous wolves enter in among you, not sparing the flock. Also of your own selves shall men arise, speaking perverse things, to draw away disciples after them. Therefore watch, and remember, that by the space of three years I ceased not to warn every one night and day with tears."

Acts 20:28-31 emphasis added.

Then the Holy Spirit said, "you stiff necked and uncircumcised in heart and ears, you do always resist the Holy Ghost: as your fathers did, so do you." Acts 7:51 Emphasis Added.

This is sad that this rebellion has been the same for many years without harmony. But that's ok, here is a scripture showing us what's really going on concerning all enemies. For it is written: "But every man in his own order: Christ the first fruits; afterward they that are Christ's at his coming. Then comes the end, when he (Jesus) shall have delivered up the kingdom to God, even the Father; when he shall have put down all rule and all authority and power. For he must reign, till he has put all enemies under his feet. The last enemy that shall be destroyed is death."

1 Corinthians 15:23-26 emphasis added.

In showing those accounts, It's imperative that I talk about what's going on in our day and age, of a matter of "certain groups of African Americans-saying they are indeed the true Hebrew Israelites of the bible. I feel discussion is necessary in this book; to help as many of them as I can.

I believe it was the Lord Jesus the Christ; that gave this topic to be recorded in this book. I'm not sure if you the reader have been hearing the hear-say that "some of the African Americans" are supposedly waking up to who they are, they believe they are "Yahweh's true Israelite people" of the Holy Bible. That they indeed are the true Hebrews, of the tribe of Juda that was scattered throughout the Earth because of their Fathers disobedience to

God.

These individuals also claim that Jesus who they say is pronounced " Yeshua" only! Not Jesus, has enlightened them to do what they are doing.

Once I challenged someone that was about to believe that doctrine, not to push away the name of Jesus. I told them, I believe anyone who does that will be guilty of "blasphemy against the Holy Spirit." Seeing good things came from that name: and that they themselves, before they had this new revelation, was also saved and filled with the Holy Spirit in that name.

I also showed them how so many died under that name, and that if we all forsake the name so violently: they're saying that all have perished under falsehood, and was never saved. I even showed them 2 Peter 2:1, where it says: "there shall be false teachers among you, who privately shall bring in damnable heresies, even denying the Lord that bought (purchased, payed for) them" (emphasis added). Through this scripture I attempted to convince them that, through Peter the Holy Spirit revealed this would happen in our times.

These African Americans also believe that Jesus indeed was of their race as well: being of the linage of Abraham according to Hebrews 2:16, 17; which says: "for surely he (Jesus Christ) took not on him the nature of angels, but he took on him the seed of Abraham. Wherefore in all things it behooved, (or was essential) to him to be made like to his brethren, that he might be a merciful and faithful high priest in things pertaining to God, to make reconciliation for the sins of the people."

They believe in this racial profile, even though scripture plainly tell us: "Though we have known Christ after the flesh, yet now henceforth know we him no more."

2 Corinthians 5:16 emphasis added.

For the scriptures are clear that says "He came to his own, and his own received him not." John 1:11 But yet says: "we henceforth know Christ no longer after the flesh;" seeing he's now made a quickening spirit. Apart from sinful flesh.

I believe these individuals; will in no doubt be fulfilling this scripture: "Now as Jannes and Jambres withstood Moses, so do these also resist the truth: men of corrupt minds, reprobate concerning the faith."

2 Timothy 3: 8 emphasis added.

For this African American race of people today to claim that they're awakening to who they truly are, and that the race of people that are now currently living in Jerusalem / Israel are not the true race, but imposters. This is a marvelous thing, that they're claiming to be the very race that all humanity blame to have crucified the savior of the World. And not only that, but this race of people are claiming to be the Children of the Nation that rejected their Messiah, and was blinded and scattered by Yahweh until the fullness of the Gentiles come to pass.

For it is written: For I would not brethren, that you should be ignorant of this mystery, unless you should be wise in your own conceits; that blindness in part is happened to Israel, until the fullness of the Gentiles be come in. Romans 11:25 Emphasis Added. Seeing this is truth, then it's time that they put away their stiff necked behavior: repent greatly, be converted before time runs out.

On another note, on the subject of his race. By the Samaritan Woman's quote at Jacobs well, that he, (Jesus) was indeed from her description a Jew, or a Judean, as stated in John 4:9. Also when Pilate asked was he the "King of the Jews" or Judeans, He didn't deny it, as stated in Mark 15:2 Amplified Bible.

"And Pilate inquired of him, are you the King of the Jews, or Judeans? And he (Christ) replied, ``It is as you Say."

I also want to add that the belief in the word "Jew" is in error, based on the fact that there weren't any books written to the Jews.

I do believe that it was to be Judean, because of what's written in Matthew 2:4-5 which says, "And when he (Herod) had gathered all the chief priests and scribes of the people together, he demanded of them where Christ should be born. And they said unto him, In Bethlehem of Judaea: for thus it is written by the prophet, "And you Bethlehem, in the land of Judah, are not the least among the princes of Judah: for out of you shall come a Governor, that shall rule my people Israel."

Seeing this scripture says: that Jesus as Governor shall rule them, this would make him (King of Judaea) as scripture records in verse 5 of that same chapter.

The people from the land of Judaea obviously spoke the Hebrew language, seeing the four gospels record that a sign was fastened above the head of Jesus crucified body which said, "This is the king of the Jews" - written in letters of- Greek, and Latin and Hebrew.

I believe that whoever was present at the crucifixion was surely one of these denominations. It holds true that for the attendees to be able to read what was inscribed. It says nothing of the "Jewish race" that spoke Yiddish, Not to include that there is a book to the Hebrews in the Holy Bible, and not to the Jews.

Marks gospel should read this way, in chapter 15 verse 2. "And Pilate asked Jesus, are you the King of the Judeans? And he answering said unto him, it is as you say." It's simple math -but easy to be agreed upon, unless you're not willing to search it out or full of debate.

One thing I do know is that the true rebellious Nation that lived in the land was surely cast out, for it is written:
"Then let them which are in Judea flee (Run) to the mountains; and let them which are in the midst of it depart out; and let not them that are in the countries enter thereunto. For these be the days of vengeance, that all things which are written may be fulfilled. But woe unto them that are with child, and to them that give suck, in those days! for there shall be great distress in the land, and wrath upon this people. And they shall fall by the edge of the sword, and shall be led away captive into all nations: and Jerusalem shall be trodden down of the Gentiles, until the times of the Gentiles be fulfilled.

The true question is, what is truly going on in Bible prophecy? Did you all know that there was twelve tribes that was scattered? For it is written:
"James, a servant of God and of the Lord Jesus Christ, to the twelve tribes which are scattered abroad, greeting." James 1:1 Emphasis Added.

Who are these one race Gentiles claiming to be the Jews of the Bible? Who ever they are, they only have but so long to occupy the land, seeing it is written again: "Therefore say, Thus saith the Lord GOD; I will even gather you from the people, and assemble you out of the countries where you have been scattered, and I will give you the land of Israel. And they shall come thither, and they shall take away all the detestable things thereof and all the abominations thereof from there." "The LORD also shall roar out of Zion, and utter his voice from Jerusalem; and the heavens and the earth shall shake: but the LORD will be the hope of his people, and the strength of the children of Israel. So shall you know that I am the LORD your God dwelling in Zion, my holy mountain: then shall Jerusalem be holy, and there shall no strangers pass through her any more.

Luke 21: 21-24 / Ezekiel 11:17-18 Joel 3:16-17 Emphasis Added.

9 REJECT SONS OF GOD

"The kings of the earth set themselves, and the rulers (the Lords), take counsel together against the LORD (Yahweh), and against his anointed (Messiah), saying, Let us break their bands (their restraints) asunder, and cast away their cords from us." Psalm 2:2, 3 emphasis added.

This is amazing insight – That these Kings and Rulers of the Earth (then and now) still have this same attitude towards their Creator, seeing not many spiritual leaders follow his word line upon line. Though many wouldn't agree to this from their own mouths, that they possess these ill, inward, rebellious desires! Our God knows who is who, who's all knowing. He knows every single Soul, how we are and how they have definitely changed on him. The reason I said this is because, not many people today are following the instructions of the Lord Jesus Christ.

If our God were to allow every single Soul free access into his great Eternal house without going through his sanctifying process, it would be a big mess and the need to have to cast out more into outer darkness or to the lower parts of the earth.

I believe, this is why the road to life is so narrow: to where few will find it, and why humanity is so scrutinized, proven and constantly tried.

For the rebellious still say today, in their hearts: "Let us break their bands (their restraints) asunder, and cast away their cords from us."
These are words of rebellion and a complete overthrow. What we have here are offspring's of God saying this, not created beings such as ministering Angels. These offspring's of God take council together to overthrow their Father, for scripture records that Jesus is the first born among many brethren. See: Romans 8:29 and Hebrews 2:10.

Here's more scriptural proof:

"But Pilate answered them, saying, Will you that I release to you the King of the Jews? For he knew that the chief priests had delivered him for envy." Mark 15:9,10 emphasis added.

"He (Jesus) said therefore, a certain nobleman went into a far country to receive for himself a kingdom, and to return. And he called his ten servants, and delivered them ten pounds, and said to them, Occupy till I come. But his citizens hated him, and sent a message after him, saying, we will not have this man to reign over us." Luke 19:12-14 emphasis added.

Though many today will not honestly admit that they fall into this category of rebels, the evidence is in our actions of not, heeding The words of Christ Jesus and following them line upon line. Our God has made it very clear and has shown us undeniable evidence that his son is real, by showing us today Miracles and healings performed in his son's name. By showing us that, we are without excuse not to follow him. But Jesus said, "If I (Jesus) had not done among them the works which none other man did, they had not had sin: but now have they both seen and hated both me and my Father." John 15:24 emphasis added.

Be it known unto all who read or hear these words, that for many years our Forefathers have been a stiff neck rebellious house, provoking Yahweh to a jealous wrath." If any have a question of why few are saved? Then let this serve as your complete answer.

This is also why I believe it's recorded: "Again, the kingdom of heaven is like a net, which was cast into the sea, and gathered of every kind: Which, when it was full, they drew to the shore, and sat down, and gathered the good into vessels, but cast away the bad." By showing all these scriptures, it's so you also who's reading this will examine yourselves not to fall in this number of, "rejected   Sons   of   God."

10 GOD SENDING PEOPLE TO HELL

Why would God send people to hell to burn for Eternity? Why such a harsh judgment on fallen souls?

First of all, anyone who's waiting on an answer to this question, must first get out of their thinking, that these are just mere people going to hell. These are not just mere people as we have come to know, who live on earth. These are god's, yes all are god's. For it is written in John 10:34. "Jesus answered them, Is it not written in your law, I said, You are gods?" And, 1 Corinthians 8:5 says: "For though there be that are called gods, whether in heaven or in earth, (as there be gods many, and lords many). Acts 17:28 says, "For in him (Yahweh) we live, and move, and have our being; as certain also of your own poets have said, For we are also his offspring." I pray these scriptures brought some light on who we really are, apart from what we were taught. As you read on, I pray these next scriptures open your eyes as they did my own.
"And the LORD said, Behold, the people is one, and they have all one language; and this they begin to do: (The Tower) and now nothing will be restrained from them, which they have imagined to do. Go to, let us go down, and there confound their language, that they may not understand one another's speech."
Genesis 11:6, 7 emphasis added.

Based on that scripture, and Matthew 25:41. I believe this is why "Hell / The Lake of fire," was prepared for the devil (Satan) and his angels, and now cursed souls of Mankind. All Souls who follow Satan's pattern, will no doubt receive the same punishment, seeing they heard of the light and truth of God but refused to follow it as Satan did.

I'm going to use the example of Prisoners locked up behind bars, that can't function in society. As criminals, insane people are locked up to keep the peace and a functional society, so to must spiritual rebels be put away as well. You, as well as I, know that they have been known to break out at times. Well, So also would spiritual rebels do the same. So seeing that these Spirits can't die as he their creator can't die, they who would go against Heavenly Government must now face godlike imprisonment as well, with no chances to escape.

They as offspring's of God, being little god's, ever exist as well, to think and do as they please. Seeing this is true, all rebels of this sort, must be put in constant torment, unless they sit, plot and plan as one force, to escape. Then later seek to overthrow or pollute the new earth and Heavenly Government. I wish this wasn't so – but unfortunately that's the way it has to be.

Once, when I was comparing the biblical account of the rich man talking to Abraham in hell, verse the biblical account Jesus revealed of the torment in the lake / furnace or outer darkness.

I noticed that in He'll it was shown people are allowed to talk and make requests, but in the lake of fire, the furnace or outer darkness, the damned Souls could only weep, cry while gnashing or grinding their teeth. I noticed first that this must be explained in detail to cause us to avoid it at all cost, and or to show us, truly there isn't any conversations there at all.

It seems very harsh, but for the sake of keeping the peace, it's understandable to me, our God is a just God giving everyone what they truly deserve. True and righteous are his ways and his wisdom is unsearchable. By hearing this, let us all have a moment of silence to think on our ways and repent if needs be, to possibly escape a horrible destructive eternal future.

11 WORD OF WARNING

Our God knows the power of oneness. He would prefer if we all desired to carry out his righteous cause, but unfortunately that isn't true. He knows that even in the new Heaven and new Earth, that without a reminder, the "free will" may have a chance of changing on him again. This scripture was shown to me as well to answer that question.

"For as the new heavens and the new earth, which I will make, shall remain before me, says the LORD, so shall your seed and your name remain. And it shall come to pass, that from one new moon to another, and from one Sabbath to another, shall all flesh come to worship before me, says the LORD. And they shall go forth, and look upon the carcasses of the men that have transgressed against me: for their worm shall not die, neither shall their fire be quenched; and they shall be an abhorring unto all flesh." Isaiah 66:22-24 emphasis added.

The reason this says "the carcasses of men" and not of god's is because of what Psalm 82:6-7 explains. For it is written;
"I (The Lord) have said, You are gods; and all of you are children of the most High. But you shall die like men, and fall like one of the princes." Emphasis on, " you shall die like men."

 This is a horrible scene, but very much necessary seeing our God is a Just God. I encourage everyone who should read these pages to take another view on life, unless most of us be set as a gazing stock for all eternity in the lake of fire.

Most have said they would obey and serve God throughout eternity – but fail to see that it starts here on Earth – while we have breath in our lungs. for I am persuaded the Lord is still saying: "Let them shout for joy, and be glad, that favor my righteous cause: yes, let them say continually, let the LORD be magnified, which has pleasure in the prosperity of his servant." Psalms 35:27 emphasis added.

The Holy Bible is a just instrument itself: showing us what was, and is, and yet to come. We're all without excuse, just as the Generation that Christ openly spoke to, concerning seeing the things they saw but repented not. He says,

"And you, Capernaum, which are exalted to heaven, shall be brought down to hell: for if the mighty works which have been done in you, had been done in Sodom, it would have remained until this day."

It's a great thing: that there are Souls that would hate, and envy, and go against their creator. Here we have Jesus coming to his own people as a forerunner, as a pattern to his brethren of what the Father expects of all his Sons, but they refused to humble themselves and follow instructions. Instead of doing that, they decided not to allow anyone to lead them, but to be their own gods,
fulfilling their own wills and agendas. This is why I believe it's written, "And it shall come to pass, that every soul, which will not hear that prophet (Jesus Christ), shall be destroyed from among the people." Acts 3:23 emphasis added.

But for hope and a remedy, the Heavenly Father says through his Son: "Whoever therefore shall humble himself as this little child, the same is greatest in the kingdom of heaven." And also, "Incline your ear, and come unto me: hear, and your soul shall live; and I will make an everlasting covenant with you, even the sure mercies of David." Matthew 18:4 / Isaiah 55:3 Emphasis added.

Furthermore it is written, "At that time Jesus answered and said, I thank you, O Father, Lord of heaven and earth, because you have hid these things from the wise and prudent, and have revealed them to babes. Matthew 11:25 emphasis added.

I believe, for God to say and record that, we're to be "humble as a child," to be great in his eyes, he knows something we don't. Only the humble is exalted and the proud is brought low, no one will ascend to the heavenly realm having a stiff necked, unjust attitude. For scripture records Heaven as such:

"To the general assembly and church of the firstborn, which are written in heaven, and to God the Judge of all, and to the spirits of just men made perfect." Hebrews 12:23 emphasis on "just men."

Here's another example in scripture of who our God doesn't want us to be like. Paul said, "I wrote to the church: but Diotrephes, who loves to have the preeminence (have leadership) does not receive us. Wherefore, if I come, I will remember his deeds which he do, prating (boiling over) against us with malicious words: and not content therewith, neither does he himself receive the brethren, and forbid them that would, and cast them out of the church.

Beloved, follow not that which is evil, but that which is good. He that do good is of God: but he that do evil has not seen God.
3 John 1: 9-11 Emphasis added.

Jesus said: "But when the husbandmen saw the son, they said among themselves, "This is the heir; come, let us kill him, and let us seize on his inheritance. And they caught him, and cast him out of the vineyard, and killed him."
Matthew 21:38, 39

And the next Sabbath day came almost the whole city together to hear the word of God. But when the Jews saw the multitudes, they were filled with envy, and spoke against those things which were spoken by Paul, contradicting and blaspheming. Then Paul and Barnabas waxed bold, and said, it was necessary that the word of God should first have been spoken to you: but seeing you put it from you, and judge yourselves unworthy of everlasting life, lo, we turn to the Gentiles.

Why do the heathen rage, and the people imagine a vain thing? The Kings of the earth set themselves, and the rulers take counsel together, against the LORD, and against his anointed, (his Christ) Psalms 2: 1, 2 Acts 4:25, 26 emphasis added.

Here we can clearly see a people that constantly agree together to go against the grain – one clear proof we have that these things are true is because our God cannot lie – this is what he see in different individuals – seeing this book is entitled " Understanding and Knowing God" – we who read these pages should see why the Godhead chose to record these events, and different characters. I have to constantly use Bible verses to prove to you, (the reader) that these things are indeed written true, as hard as it is to believe. We should pause and think on these things a while before reading on.

Most people that don't know the Godhead, are convinced that they're not fair, not right, and basically they're not who they want them to be. Ultimately it was necessary to record these topics, for they are definitely needed in this strange, deceitful World we live in.

This World is full of images (and words) to download into the hearts & minds of mankind, to influence some to want power and position, not having to be subject to anyone dictating them.
For instance: these "Marvel & DC Comic book characters," that's brought to life in theaters, show images of little gods living independent lives with no one to answer to. I feel These Movies are a tactic of our adversary the

devil, to put in our minds - to want that power and independence outside of this life. This type of thinking goes contrary to what the Holy Bible teaches, actually the bible says most won't be able to adhere to the requirement of thriving in God's Kingdom, let alone, to be promoted to a place of position and authority.

This   Topic   leads   to   the   next   question.

12 WHAT DOES GOD WANT FROM ME?

What is it God wants from me? Why so many rules? why can't I just live like I want to and still be accepted of him?

Here's a few scriptures that might help to answer "what God wants from you? "Then spake Jesus again to them, saying, I am the light of the world: he that follows me shall not walk in darkness, but shall have the light of life." John 8:12 emphasis added.

Walking in darkness is a heart condition – If our Spirits are corrupted then the darkness in us is great – Only by being joined to Jesus Spirit are we able to walk in the light.

Jesus put it this way - " If you then being evil know how to give good gifts to your children, how much more shall your Father who is in heaven give good things to them that ask him? " The emphasis is on "humanity being evil, apart from God the Father who is Holy.

Jesus then went on to say:

"The light of the body is the eye(or Spirit), therefore when your eye (or Spirit) is single, your whole body also is full of light; but when your eye (or Spirit) is evil, your body also is full of darkness. I believe the Lord brought clarity to me about this scripture, showing me that: Seeing humanity by nature are considered evil apart from him and the Father, That in order to have that light of the body, we need to be joined to him and the Father who is one. For the scriptures say: "But he that is joined to the Lord is one spirit." And, "He God is in one mind, and who can turn him? And that: We have the mind of Christ." 1 Corinthians 6:17 / Job 23: 13 / 1 Corinthians 2:16 Emphasis Added.

We all should share the same Spirit between us-this explains our eye being single. That's how were able to know what God feels and what he is saying to us (collectively) - So to say: "What is it God wants from me" – he wants you as a bride in the Spirit – whether Male or Female – He's the lover of our Souls – This is what the word of God has to say concerning his plan for us.

For it is written: "That he (Christ) might present it (or you) to himself a glorious church, not having spot, or wrinkle, or any such thing; but that it should be holy and without blemish." Ephesians 5:27

His thoughts went on to say about us:

"But you are a chosen generation, a royal priesthood, a holy nation, a peculiar people; that you should show forth the praises of him who has called you out of darkness into his marvelous light:" 1 Peter 2:9 emphasis added.

This is what he wants from us, I'm convinced we are capable of doing our part, seeing he is God and he saw this in us. He said, "we are as he is in this present world." It's simple, he's a set apart (Holy) God; and commands that we all stay set apart from this filthy world system, and the sins that accompany it, for it is written:

"And we know that we are of God, and the whole world lies in wickedness. "
1 John 5:19 emphasis added.

There are many, many more scriptures confirming what our God wants from us – he indeed will give us his grace to live a Holy life – if we cooperate with him – we must put our trust in him – we cannot do this in our own strength - for without him we can do nothing – we are to live in who he is - and will remain to be - that's a God of love, compassion and purity - in and through us to humanity.

This is what our God wants, he wants
Christ be formed in us, Galatians 4:19. and to say, "why so many rules?" I say what rules? Do you mean commandments? If so then, this is what the Bible has to say about that in 1 John 5:3 Amplified version.
"For the [true] love of God is this: that we do His commands [keep His ordinances and are mindful of His precepts and teaching]. And these orders of His are not irksome (burdensome, oppressive, or grievous).

For if you didn't know, Jesus made things lighter for us, for it is written: "Let no man therefore judge you in meat, or in drink, or in respect of an holyday, or of the new moon, or of the Sabbath days: Which are a shadow of things to come; but the body is of Christ." Then Jesus showed to all now in the new covenant, about what works to do. For it is written: "Then said they unto him, What shall we do, that we might work the works of God? Jesus answered and said unto them, This is the work of God, that you believe on him whom he has sent." Colossians 2:16-17 John 6:28-29 emphasis added.

Jesus pleased the Heavenly Father for us, now we are only required to do the "least commandments."

Lastly, the question to you is, how do you want to live? What does it Intel? If it's your way of doing things, then your way is the wrong way, and will only lead you down a dark path. If it's God's way then it will lead you to safety. For it is written: For all that is in the world, the lust of the flesh, and the lust of the eyes, and the pride of life, is not of the Father, but is of the world. And the world is passing away, and the lust thereof: but he that continues to do the will of God continues to abide for ever. 1 John 2:16-17 emphasis added.

Our God wants remaining fruit in our lives, seeing we are described in his eyes being "trees of righteousness." For it is written:
"Blessed is the man that does not walk in the counsel of the ungodly, a nor continue to stand in the way of sinners, nor continue to sit in the seat of the scornful. But his delight is in the law (or the word) of the Lord ; and in his law (do) he meditate day and night. And he shall be like a tree planted by the rivers of water, that continue to bring forth his fruit in his season; his leaf also shall not wither; and whatsoever he continues to do shall prosper." Psalm 1:1-3 emphasis added. This is one of many things our God wants from us.

Jesus said it this way: "Come to me, all you that labor and are heavy laden, and I will give you rest. Take my yoke upon you, and learn from me: for I am meek and lowly in heart: and you shall find rest to your souls. For my yoke is easy, (better) and my burden is light" (becoming light bearers). Matthew 11: 28-30 emphasis added.

I believe he said this, so we would compare what he's asking, to the yoke of the old traditions, and our experience of carrying the yoke of being slaves to sin. For us to say there are too many rules, it isn't that much as in comparison to the many instructions of the old covenant - which no one could do or keep.

Scripture records that we were born in sin, made in iniquity, until Christ came to set us all free from such bondage because of the fall of the first Man and Woman.

Seeing we are not programmed robots, but free to think and serve God if we want to or not. It shouldn't be a great surprise to know that God must put rules in place to test man, to see if would just follow them willingly. He does help us along the way. Scripture records that God deals with man, but yet helps man, as it is written.

"For God speaks once, yes twice, yet man perceive it not. In a dream, in a vision of the night, when deep sleep falls upon men, in slumbering upon the bed; then he (The Most High) - opens the ears of men, and seals their instruction, that he may withdraw man from his purpose, and hide pride from man. He keeps back his soul from the pit, and his life from perishing by the sword. He (That Soul) shall pray unto God, and he (God) will be favorable unto him: and he shall see his face with joy: for he will render unto man his righteousness. He looks upon men, and if any say, "I have sinned, and perverted that which was right, and it profited me not;" He (God) will deliver his soul from going into the pit, and his life shall see the light. Lo, all these things work God oftentimes with man, to bring back his soul from the pit, to be enlightened with the light of the living." Job 33:14-18 emphasis added.

When I saw this, I was in Awe of God who would so love us, and order our steps that we don't perish so quickly. For indeed he desires to help us and teach us of his ways.

FOR IT IS WRITTEN & SPOKEN OUT OF THE MOUTH OF TWO PROPHETS

"And many people shall go and say, come you, and let us go up to the mountain of the LORD, to the house of the God of Jacob; and he will teach us of his ways, and we will walk in his paths: for out of Zion shall go forth the law, and the word of the LORD from Jerusalem." Isaiah 2:3 emphasis added.

"And many nations shall come, and say, Come, and let us go up to the mountain of the LORD, and to the house of the God of Jacob; and he will teach us of his ways, and we will walk in his paths: for the law shall go forth of Zion, and the word of the LORD from Jerusalem."
Micah 4:2 emphasis added.

This is a marvelous thing, that our God would show us future events that's to take place before they happen.

There are a lot of Souls who just wander through life, making life what they want it to be. Guessing from day to day, following other influential men or women to do their agendas. But since I have been alive, I haven't seen or heard of a Government that's continuing to walk in, or follow Gods ways. Even Churches in every Country are divided, and don't necessarily follow a pattern of divine setup, to continue in it.

It seems, it's an individual thing we have to do. For when groups of people got together sharing the same interest, it appears that is where the rise of different religions came from. But if you ask me, we are all without excuse, seeing our God simplified his requirements in the words of Christ to follow them.

So to say, "there are too many rules," I can't agree, our God knows what we're capable of; we know good from evil. We would do well to take heed to his simple instructions, to do them. I also observe how we as humanity, go about our day, being side-tracked a lot with entertainment of all sorts. We rarely have time, or bring up the discussion of the true meaning of life according to the Holy Bible to our own misfortune.

I guess we've also become accustomed to being undercover with our religious beliefs as well, when it comes to political or social interactions, we come alive, it's a whole other story. But that's why I'm hoping this book would be a blessing to awaken some: to rethink this life, and divorce their own beliefs, to search out the Holy Bible for themselves - for more unanswered questions about the true meaning of life, and who our God is, and what he require of us to do.

I can't agree that all Nations on Earth will repent and walk in his ways, but according to prophecy, things will get worse before they get better, but for us who are true believers Philippians 1:6 is our future. For it is written: "Being confident of this very thing, that he which hath begun a good work in you will perform it until the day of Jesus Christ."

13 SOME WON'T MAKE HEAVEN

Why do the bible say so many in the Church will not make heaven?

The bible records different reasons many people won't make heaven – but I feel impressed to share this scripture as one focal point – seeing it is a glimpse into the future of the final judgment:

Jesus says it this way. "And why call you me, Lord, Lord, and do not the things which I say?" "Not everyone that say unto me, Lord, Lord, shall enter into the kingdom of heaven; but he that do the will of my Father which is in heaven. Many will say to me in that day, Lord, Lord, have we not prophesied in your name? And in your name have cast out devils? And in your name, done many wonderful works? And then will I profess unto them, I never knew you: depart from me, you that work iniquity, (Lawlessness)." Luke 6:46 / Matthew 7:22 emphasis added.

Notice how the Lord said: we have to do the will of the Father? If stiff necked people can't humble themselves to do another's will; how can they expect to be accepted by him. He will not allow them the chance to be Rebels.

Jesus also said "I never knew you." Here's a scripture that many seem to overlook – but it carries weight in explaining why the Lord would say "I never knew you."

"When once the master of the house is risen up, and has shut to the door, and you begin to stand without, and to knock at the door, saying, Lord, Lord, open unto us; and he shall answer and say unto you, I know you not who you are: then shall you begin to say, we have eaten and drank in your presence, and you have taught in our streets. But he shall say, I tell you, I know you not who you are; depart from me, all you workers of iniquity."
Luke 13: 25- 27 emphasis added.

"And John answered Jesus, saying, Master, we saw one casting out demons in your name, and he follow not us: and we forbad (stopped) him, because he follow not us. But Jesus said, forbid him not: for there is no man which shall do a miracle in my name that can lightly speak evil of me."
Mark 9:38, 39 emphasis added.

Notice how the disciples said "he doesn't follow us" If this person didn't follow Jesus then how would Jesus get to know him – but yet the man was casting out a demon in his name.

We also must keep in mind the scripture also say: "For the gifts and callings of God are without repentance. (irrevocable) and let God be true, but every man a liar."
Romans 11: 29 / Romans 3: 4 emphasis added.

Even though the other Individuals saw Jesus personally, dined with him, and even heard his teachings, it didn't matter. Jesus still said, "I don't know you who you are." Here we can see a picture of people doing the work and people just sitting listening. It doesn't matter who we are, we have to make sure Jesus knows us.

This is what the bible say concerning Jesus knowing us: he still says- "My sheep hear my voice, and I know them, and they follow me; and - if any man loves God, the same is known of him."
John 10:27 / 1 Corinthians 8: 3 emphasis added.

When people first come into the Kingdom of God, it seems mediocre, or that's what Certain Preachers make it out to be. When they shouldn't spare the words of Christ from the Father, to warn them.

People go to Churches listening to differing sermons, not knowing they are giving heed to seducing spirits, and doctrines of devils. These places are full of people (Having itching ears, directing them to do this or that, when People fail to read the Bible for themselves. For example, scriptures on what the future entails about their walk with Christ, and that there are opponents to our faith, including our own outward nature that we have to die to.

That's why Paul wrote: "For we know that the law is spiritual: but I am carnal, sold under sin. For that which I want to do, I allow not: for what I should do, that I do not do; but what I hate, that I do.
If then I do that which I don't want to do, I consent to the law that it is good. Now then it is no more I that do it, but sin that dwells in me. For I know that in me (that is, in my flesh,) dwells no good thing: for will power is present with me; but how to perform that which is good, I find not.

For the good that I should do, I do not: but the evil which I shouldn't do, that I do. Now if I do that I shouldn't, it is no more I that do it, but sin that dwells in me. I find then a law, that, when I would do good, evil is present with me. For I delight in the law of God after the inward man: But I see another law in my members, warring against the law of my mind, and bringing me into captivity to the law of sin which is in my members.

O wretched man that I am! Who shall deliver me from the body of this death? I thank God – It's through Jesus Christ our Lord. So then with the mind I myself serve the law of God; but with the flesh the law of sin.

There is therefore now no condemnation to them which are in Christ Jesus, who walk not after the flesh, but after the Spirit. For the law of the Spirit of life in Christ Jesus has made me free from the law of sin and death. For what the law could not do, in that it was weak through the flesh, God sending his own Son in the likeness of sinful flesh, and for sin, condemned sin in the flesh: That the righteousness of the law might be fulfilled in us, who walk not after the flesh, but after the Spirit. And they that are Christ's have crucified the flesh with the affections and lusts.

Romans 7:14-24 8: 1-4 / Galatians 5:24 emphasis added.

Also a lot of people won't make it because they will not be able to endure the "baptism with fire." This Baptism of fire will prove everyone, for it is also written, "That the trial of your faith, being much more precious than of gold that perishes, though it be tried with fire, might be found unto praise and honor and glory at the appearing of Jesus Christ." And also, "I (The Lord) will bring the third part through the fire, and will refine them as silver is refined, and will try them as gold is tried: they shall call on my name, and I will hear them: I will say, It is my people: and they shall say, The LORD is my God". 1 Peter 1:7 / Zechariah 13:9 emphasis added.

All in all every one of us must be proven by the Most High, even those who will come into the kingdom in the last days. For it is written, "Many shall be purified, and made white, and tried; but the wicked shall do wickedly: and none of the wicked shall understand; but the wise shall understand." Daniel 12:10 emphasis added.

No one should boast – but remain unmovable in this walk with Christ – he knew and still knows of individuals that would turn back or be deceived – this is why he says: "Nevertheless the foundation of God stands sure, having this seal, the Lord knows them that are his. And let everyone that name the name of Christ depart from iniquity." And also:

"Then shall the kingdom of heaven be likened to ten virgins, who took their lamps, and went forth to meet the bridegroom. And five of them were wise, and five were foolish." Emphasis added. Read this account for yourselves, to see why the Lord Jesus said, "five were foolish."

2 Timothy 2:9 / Matthew 25:1, 2 emphasis added.

This is why we should all get married to Christ Jesus, through an Audible, vocal confession, receive his Holy Spirit, then read the Bible for ourselves, so we won't be led astray. That's why it is written. "You therefore, beloved, seeing you know these things before, beware unless you also, being led away with the error of the wicked, fall from your own steadfastness." And also,

"The grace of the Lord Jesus Christ, and the love of God, and the communion of the Holy Ghost, be with you all. Amen."

2 Peter 3:17 / 2 Corinthians 13:14 emphasis added.

For it is written," I (John) indeed baptize you with water to repentance: but he (The Christ) that comes after me is mightier than I, whose shoes I am not worthy to bear: he shall baptize you with the Holy Spirit, and with fire: Whose fan (Winnowing Fork) is in his hand, and he will thoroughly (purge, cleanse) his floor, and gather his wheat into the granary; but he will burn the chaff with unquenchable fire. Some may ask, what is this fire?

That's a good question. This is what I asked at one time myself, until I found out this was written. "Beloved, think it not strange concerning the fiery trial which is to try you, as though some strange thing happened to you." "But he that received the seed (the word) into stony places, the same is he that hear the word, and (immediately) with joy receive it; yet he has not root in himself, but (remain) for a while: for when tribulation or persecution arise because of the word, immediately he is offended.

1 Peter 4:12 and Matthew 13:20, 21 emphasis added.

IN OTHER WORDS, IT'S NOT HOW WE START, IT'S HOW WE'LL FINISH, FOR EVEN THE DEVIL STARTED OUT RIGHT!

These scriptures are one in the same, He has said, and is still saying that he will purge and refine these individuals to utter perfection, making Individuals just like himself.

For example, when gold is in its purest state, the refiner is able to see his or her own facial image in it, (like a mirror). This is the Almighty Father's will, for it is written, "For whom he (Jehovah) did foreknow, he also did predestinate to be conformed to the image of his Son, (Jesus) that he might be the firstborn among many brethren." Romans 8:29 emphasis added.

14 GOD DIDN'T PROTECT MY CHILD

Why didn't God protect my child from dying while I was serving him?

This is a sensitive question – I have in fact wandered the same about this statement; – but I assure you, – the Bible has a lot of examples of men and women that lost Children for different reasons.

It seems this question was asked of a Minister: because the question states, "While I was serving God."

Before I get into this answer, It's imperative that we examine this scripture first which says. "He that love father or mother more than me is not worthy of me: and he that love son or daughter more than me is not worthy of me." Matthew 10:37 (Emphasis added).

Since we're on the subject of a minister's child dyeing: let's focus in on "he that love son or daughter more than me is not worthy of me." Doesn't this sound like, "Gods rules of engagement?" Before anyone was to follow Christ, he or she were to careful consider this possibility; knowing what enemy they were engaging. Also remember God also says, "For my thoughts are not your thoughts, neither are your ways my ways, says the LORD. For as the heavens are higher than the earth, so are my ways higher than your ways, and my thoughts than your thoughts." Isaiah 55:8, 9 emphasis added.

We all have to keep this in mind as we explore to know our God- the only thing we have is his Holy Spirit and his word to give us insight – let's explore this question in two parts first.

"Why didn't God protect my child from dying?"

Of course in a perfect world – we as humans would want this in our perfect World – but unfortunately this isn't reality,   only in the world to come Eternal life does the Bible record things like this. "And the sucking child shall play on the hole of the asp (Cobra) and the weaned child shall put his hand on the cockatrice' (Viper's) den. They shall not hurt nor destroy in all my holy mountain: for the earth shall be full of the knowledge of the LORD, as the waters cover the sea. Isaiah 11:8-9 emphasis added.

Scripture records: Wherefore, as by one man, sin entered into the world, and death by sin; and so death passed upon all men, for that all have sinned: Romans 5:12 emphasis on "sin entered into the world."

Plus the Earth is under a curse, as Revelation 22:3 shows it to be lifted. It is written. "And there shall be no more curse: but the throne of God and of the Lamb shall be in it; and his servants shall serve him." Emphasis added.

The answer is simply this, sin and a curse is causing death to come upon: young and old, small and great, it has no respect to persons, and we as adults have to be careful we're walking in wisdom from day to day, being careful not to make bad choices.

Scripture also address Children passed the age of accountability this way.

"Children, obey your parents in the Lord: for this is right. Honor your father and mother; (which is the first commandment with promise, that it may be well with you, and you may live long on the earth."

I'm not saying here all kids haven't obeyed their parents to cause death – but if you put these two scriptures together it paints a clear picture that death came either by sin or disobedience.

Let's explore a child dying case in the life of Christ. And, behold, there came one of the rulers of the synagogue, Jairus by name; and when he saw Jesus, he fell at his feet, and besought him greatly, saying, my little daughter lies at the point of death: I pray you, come and lay your hands on her, that she may be healed; and she shall live. While he yet spoke, there came from the ruler of the synagogue's house certain which said, your daughter is dead: why trouble you the Master any further? As soon as Jesus heard the word that was spoken, he said to the ruler of the synagogue, be not afraid, only believe. And when Jesus was come in, he said to them, why make you this ado, (an uproar) and weep? The damsel is not dead, but sleeps. And they laughed him to scorn. But when he had put them all out, he took the father and the mother of the damsel, and them that were with him, and entered in where the damsel was lying. And he took the damsel by the hand, and said to her, Talitha cumi; which is, being interpreted, Damsel, I say to you, arise. And immediately the damsel arose, and walked; for she was of the age of twelve years. And they were astonished with a great astonishment. Mark 5:22, 23, 35-40 Emphasis Added.

The reason for showing this scripture is that, we can surely see Our God doesn't see and think as we do.

Before Christ came, no one was performing such acts of authority to bring back the dead. Jairus only heard that through Christ, the raising of the dead were even possible.

Another reason for showing this is that Christian believers are said to be able to do the same works that the Christ did – so that Jesus would be glorified in the Earth.
Read: John 14:12.

For example: Acts 9:36-42.
"Now there was at Joppa a certain disciple named Tabitha, which by interpretation is called Dorcas: this woman was full of good works and alms deeds which she did. And it came to pass in those days, that she was sick, and died: whom when they had washed, they laid her in an upper chamber. And forasmuch as Lydda was nigh to Joppa, and the disciples had heard that Peter was there, they sent unto him two men, desiring him that he would not delay to come to them. Then Peter arose and went with them. When he was come, they brought him into the upper chamber: and all the widows stood by him weeping, and showing the coats and garments which Dorcas made, while she was with them. But Peter put them all forth, and kneeled down, and prayed; and turning him to the body said, Tabitha, arise. And she opened her eyes: and when she saw Peter, she sat up. And he gave her his hand, and lifted her up, and when he had called the saints and widows, presented her alive. And it was known throughout all Joppa; and many believed in the Lord."

Unfortunately, I believe there are not enough believers walking in this power and authority, going around cancelling funeral processions as it should be. Not to cast blame, but just to shed light on the question, "why didn't God protect my child from dying?

Death will happen no doubt, but for believers of the gospel of Jesus Christ, it can be delayed and an opportunity to give God glory. We also have to keep in mind that, whatever happens on Planet Earth, it is written that we as little gods, have allowed it.

Here is scriptural proof:

The heaven, even the heavens, are the LORD'S: but the earth has he given to the children of men.
Psalms 115:16 Emphasis Added.

"And God blessed them, (Male and Female) and God said unto them, be fruitful, and multiply, and replenish the earth, and subdue it: and have dominion over the fish of the sea, and over the fowl of the air, and over every living thing that moves upon the earth."

Genesis 1:28 Emphasis Added.

This was Gods original plan for mankind, but as we know it, things didn't continue on as expected seeing Man was tricked out of his inheritance until the Christ came to restore all things.

Life as we know it is strange: and we see, hear, and read of strange things that has taken place throughout the course of time. Let's explore the case with a man named Job to help answer this question, let's see what happened when Job kids died. For it is written: "There was a man in the land of Uz, whose name was Job; and that man was perfect and upright, and one that feared God, and eschewed evil. And there were born unto him seven sons and three daughters. And the LORD said unto Satan, Have you considered my servant Job, that there is none like him in the earth, a perfect and an upright man, one that fears God, and eschews evil? Then Satan answered the LORD, and said, Do Job fear God for nothing? Have you not made an hedge about him, and about his house, and about all that he has on every side? You have blessed the work of his hands, and his substance is increased in the land. But put forth your hand now, and touch all that he has, and he will curse you to your face. And the LORD said unto Satan, Behold, all that he has is in your power; only upon himself put not forth your hand. So Satan went forth from the presence of the LORD."

Job 1:1, 2, 8-12 ,18,19 Emphasis Added.

After Satan left the presence of the Lord, this is what happened.

"While he (Job's Servant) was yet speaking, there came also another, and said, your Sons and your daughters were eating and drinking wine in their eldest brother's house: and behold, there came a great wind from the wilderness, and smote the four corners of the house, and it fell upon the young men, and they are dead; and I only am escaped alone to tell you."

I encourage you the reader to read this for yourself. But here we can see that our God chose to record the story of an upright man who didn't do any wrong but yet calamity struck his life, Job instantly lost seven Sons.

He was a minister in his day, serving the Lord, until several evil reports came his way to test his faith.

The Bible also record the conversation in the Heavenly realm- where Satan and the Creator were discussing a man named Job, and because Satan said "take away things from him, that he would then curse you to your face," did make calamity and death to be made manifest.

Also remember how this same thing happened in the days Jesus walked the Earth? It wasn't a one time event. For it is written, "And the Lord said, Simon, Simon, behold, Satan has desired to have you, that he may sift you as wheat: But I have prayed for you, that your faith fail not: and when you are converted, strengthen your brethren." Luke 22:31-32 emphasis added.

Some might probably say, "what a cruel sport," isn't that what we say?

Some are also probably saying, why would God allow Satan to do this?

But did not God say that: his thoughts were not our thoughts nor his ways our ways?

For the word of God says: "No but, O man, who are you that reply against God? Shall the thing formed say to him that formed it, why have you made me this way? Doesn't the potter have power over the clay, of the same lump to make one vessel to honor, and another to dishonor?" And also: "Do we provoke the Lord to jealousy? Are we stronger than him? 1 Corinthians 10:22 / Romans 9:20, 21 emphasis added.

For it is written again, "And he (Nebuchadnezzar) was driven from the sons of men; and his heart was made like the beasts, and his dwelling was with the wild asses: they fed him with grass like oxen, and his body was wet with the dew of heaven; till he knew that the most high God ruled in the kingdom of men, and that he appoints over it whomsoever he will.

Daniel 5:21 emphasis added.

Note: Putting all these scriptures together it's simply saying: Who are we as created beings to dare question God? Seeing we are not on his level, as the scriptures plainly puts it, we are all to know that, "It's the Most High that rules in the Kingdom of men." I'm convinced, God doesn't view death as we view death.

We view death as a bad, avoidable thing, but if we saw through the eyes of God, then maybe just maybe we would shut our mouths and thoughts down.

Here's an instance where Job got to converse with his maker. Then the LORD answered Job out of the whirlwind, and said, who is this that darkens counsel by words without knowledge? Gird up now your loins like a man; for I will demand of you, and answer you me. Where were you when I laid the foundations of the earth? Declare, if you have understanding. Job 38:1-4 Emphasis Added.

This was just one of many questions God asked Job. Scripture also record this stories outcome, saying: "Look, we count them happy which endure. You have heard of the patience of Job, and have seen the end of the Lord; that the Lord is very pitiful, and of tender mercy."
James 5:11 Emphasis Added.

Look at this account – "In those days was Hezekiah sick unto death, and the prophet Isaiah the son of Amoz came to him, and said unto him, this say the Lord, set your house in order; for you shall die, and not live."

Note: After Hezekiah got this word from the Lord he went in prayer to the Lord crying- telling him of all the things he did right in his sight – till the lord sent Isaiah back in to him to tell him that God saw his tears – and that he would heal him and add 15 years to him as well - But what Hezekiah didn't know is that God who knows all things, even the future saw a Son that would be born of Hezekiah – named Manasseh- and this is what it says of his Son:

So Manasseh made Judah and the inhabitants of Jerusalem to err, (to stray) and to do worse than the heathen, whom the Lord had destroyed before the children of Israel 2 Chronicles 33:9 Emphasis Added.

So as we can see, God doesn't see as man see's, and he doesn't always tell us of the future of why he wants people to go the way of the Earth - especially when he or she wasn't doing anything to deserve death.
For as we saw Hezekiah was doing ok in Gods sight.

For it is written again: "The righteous continues to perish, and no man continue to lay it to heart: and merciful men are taken away, none considering that the righteous is taken away from the evil to come."
Isaiah 57:1 Emphasis Added.

We don't have to fear death, for Gods word tells us: "Look, the eye of the LORD is upon them that fear him, upon them that hope in his mercy; to deliver their soul from death, and to keep them alive in famine." Psalms 33:18, 19 emphasis added.

So you see? God is in control and we as believers need to get a renewed mind concerning all things, especially on this subject of death. For it is written again: For to me to live is Christ, and to die is gain. Philippians 1:21 emphasis added.

Hear what Jesus said on this subject: "and you shall be betrayed both by parents, and brethren, and kinsfolk's, and friends; and some of you shall they

cause to be put to death. And you shall be hated of all men for my name's sake. But there shall not a hair of your head perish."
Luke 21:16-18 Emphasis Added.

And also, "Fear none of those things which you shall suffer: behold, the devil shall cast some of you into prison, that you may be tried; and you shall have tribulation ten days: be you faithful unto death, and I will give you a crown of life.
Revelation 2:10 Emphasis Added.

See how God views dyeing? He even compares it to falling asleep: "Then said Jesus disciples, Lord, if Lazarus sleeps, he shall do well. Howbeit Jesus spoke of his death: but they thought that he had spoken of taking of rest in sleep. Then said Jesus to them plainly, Lazarus is dead."
John 11:12-14 Emphasis Added.

15 BAD HAPPENING TO GOOD PEOPLE

This leads me to the next Question: Why do bad things happen to "good people?

As we saw in the last chapter in Acts 9:36-42, a certain disciple named Tabitha, which by interpretation is called Dorcas was a good person, but died. I believe this was put in the scriptures for a reason. Showing that good people who do good things can die as well as bad people.

Death comes to all in this life unless God says not so. Here's an example in scripture of God telling Death not so.

And in those days shall men seek death, and shall not find it; and shall desire to die, and death shall flee from them. Revelation 9:6 Emphasis Added.

I assure you, it's not because death can make this decision, but that the Creator says not so. Scripture records many cases of
Bad things happening to Good and bad people alike.
Here's an example of Bad things happening to good people.
"Women received their dead raised to life again: and others were tortured, not accepting deliverance; that they might obtain a better resurrection: and others (Saints) had trial of cruel mocking and scourging, yes, moreover of bonds and imprisonment: They were stoned, they were sawed in half, were tempted, were slain with the sword: they wandered about in sheepskins and goatskins; being destitute, afflicted, tormented; (Of whom the world was not worthy. They wandered in deserts, and in mountains, and in dens and caves of the earth." Hebrews 11:35-38 Emphasis Added.

"These things have I (Jesus) spoken unto you, that you should not be offended. They shall put you out of the synagogues (Churches), yes, the time will come, that whosoever kill you will think that he do God service. And these things will they do unto you, because they have not known the Father, nor me." John 16: 1- 3 emphasis added.

Remember Jesus said: "If you were of the world, the world would love his own: but because you are not of the world, but I have chosen you out of the world, therefore the world hates you."

They that are of the world, simply despise God and his people. This hatred is so severe to where, they take pleasure in killing you. But as you may know by now, they can't kill you. You can never die.

Jesus was the ultimate good person, and look at how they did him. It's just the carnal mind of Man that drives him. For it is written: "Now the mind of the flesh [which is sense and reason without the Holy Spirit] is death [death that comprises all the miseries arising from sin, both here and hereafter]. But the mind of the [Holy] Spirit is life and [soul] peace [both now and forever]. [That is] because the mind of the flesh [with its carnal thoughts and purposes] is hostile to God, for it does not submit itself to God's Law; indeed it cannot. So then those who are living the life of the flesh [catering to the appetites and impulses of their carnal nature] cannot please or satisfy God, or be acceptable to Him."
Romans 8:6-8 Amplified Bible with Emphasis Added. The Bible describes them as this: "men of the world, which have their portion in this life," Psalm 17:14 emphasis added.

But not good, born again people, they are described as this, "just men made perfect, Hebrews 12:23 Emphasis Added.

The whole reads this way: "But rather, you (who are Saints) have come to Mount Zion, even to the city of the living God, the heavenly Jerusalem, and to countless multitudes of angels in festal gathering, And to the church (assembly) of the Firstborn who are registered [as citizens] in heaven, and to the God Who is Judge of all, and to the spirits of the righteous (the redeemed in heaven) who have been made perfect.

These are all of the ones who has favored God's righteous cause, and was described as such: "My sheep hear my voice, and I (Christ Jesus) know them, and they follow me: And I give unto them eternal life; and they shall never perish, neither shall any man pluck them out of my hand. My Father, which gave them me, is greater than all; and no man is able to pluck them out of my Father's hand. I and my Father are one.
John 10:27-30 Emphasis Added.

This is a picture of them coming back, in the not so distant future. For it is written: "And Enoch also, the seventh from Adam, prophesied of these, saying, Behold, the Lord cometh with ten thousands of his saints, To execute judgment upon all, and to convince all that are ungodly among them of all their ungodly deeds which they have ungodly committed, and of all their hard speeches which ungodly sinners have spoken against him.
Jude 1:14-15 Emphasis Added.

Dear reader, we all just need a believing heart, and a renewed mind, being strong in our faith. I constantly tell everyone I talk to on this subject, I tell them , " If we don't stand for something, we will fall for anything."

We only have so much time to believe the truth of the gosple of Jesus Christ, before the Creator of all things send strong delusions to all who didn't want the love of the truth to be saved. For it is written in 2 Thessalonians 2:3-12. "Let no man deceive you by any means: for that day (The day of Jesus return) shall not come, except there come a falling away first, and that man of sin be revealed, the son of perdition (aka Antichrist); Who continue to oppose and continues to exalt himself above all that is called God, or that is worshipped; so that he as God continues to sit in the temple of God, showing himself that he is God. Remember you not, that, when I was yet with you, I told you these things? And now you know what continues to withhold that he might be revealed in his time. For the mystery of iniquity (lawlessness) does already work: only he who now continues to let (or restrain) will let (or restrain), until he be taken out of the way. And then shall that Wicked be revealed, whom the Lord shall consume with the spirit of his mouth, and shall destroy with the brightness of his coming: Even him, whose coming is after the working of Satan with all power and signs and lying wonders, And with all deceivableness of unrighteousness in them that perish; because they received not the love of the truth, that they might be saved. And for this cause God shall send them strong delusion, that they should believe a lie: That they all might be damned who believed not the truth, but had pleasure in unrighteousness.

Be warned Saints, be watchful, and whatever you do, don't charge God foolishly   because   of   a   lack   of   understanding.

16 GOD IS FATHER, WHO'S MOTHER?

If God is our Heavenly Father; who then is our Mother?

Warning! Only the spiritual minded can understand these things. The following scriptures will explain wisdom as being our Mother. For it is written: "My son, hear the instruction of your father, and forsake not the law of your mother: my son, keep your father's commandment, and forsake not the law of your mother."
Proverbs 1:8 / Proverbs 6:20 Emphasis Added.

"Wisdom cries without; she utters her voice in the streets, wisdom has built her house, she hath hewn out her seven pillars:" Proverbs 9:1 / Proverbs 1:20 emphasis added.

The Heavenly Father, by his word says: "My son keep my words, and lay up my commandments with you. Keep my commandments, and live; and my law as the apple of your eye. Bind them upon your fingers, write them upon the table of your heart. Say unto wisdom, you are my sister; and call understanding your kinswoman: that they may keep you from the strange woman, from the stranger which flatters with her words." Proverbs 7:1- 5 emphasis added.

Notice how at the end of this scripture it warns us of another Woman, apart from Mom Wisdom, to take heed and watch out for. She's called the "Strange Woman."

James 3:15, explains this Strange Woman like this: "This wisdom descends not from above, but is earthly, sensual, devilish."

Our God is Just to warn us of a Counterfeit among us, to watch out for. I believe a lot of so called inspired Men and Women are operating under this strange Woman to deceive the masses. The Woman wisdom that is from above, she's described this way. For it is written: but the wisdom that is from above is first pure, then Peaceable, gentle, and easy to be entreated, full of mercy and good fruits, without partiality, and without hypocrisy." James 3:17 emphasis added.

This plainly tells us all what to look out for, so we're not tricked. Seeing this "Strange Woman" is described as earthly, I believe she is described in scripture this way.

For it is written: "Then the angel who talked with me came forward and said to me, Lift up now your eyes and see what this is that goes forth. And I said, What is it? [What does it symbolize?] And he said, This that goes forth is an ephah [-sized vessel for separate grains all collected together]. This, he continued, is the symbol of the sinners mentioned above and is the resemblance of their iniquity throughout the whole land. And behold, a round, flat weight of lead was lifted and there sat a woman in the midst of the ephah [-sized vessel]. And he said, This is lawlessness (wickedness)! And he thrust her back into the ephah [-sized vessel] and he cast the weight of lead upon the mouth of it! Then lifted I up my eyes and looked, and behold, there were two women coming forward! The wind was in their wings, for they had wings like the wings of a stork, and they lifted up the ephah
[-sized vessel] between the earth and the heavens. Then said I to the angel who talked with me, Where are they taking the ephah [-sized vessel]? And he said to me, To the land of Shinar [Babylonia] to build it a house, and when it is finished, to set up the ephah [-sized vessel — the symbol of such sinners and their guilt] there upon its own base."

Beware Saints of this Woman called Lawlessness / Wickedness. She's destined to overthrow any and all who's not ordained to Eternal Life.

The Apostle Paul mentioned the true spirit of wisdom when he said: "That the God of our Lord Jesus Christ, the Father of glory, may give unto you the spirit of wisdom and revelation in the knowledge of him:" Ephesians 1:17 emphasis added.

Here's the mentioning of the Seven Spirits of God that John (in the book of Revelation) wrote about, that still rests upon the Lord Jesus Christ, and his true servants.

For it is written: "The spirit of the Lord shall rest upon him (Jesus), the spirit of wisdom and understanding, the spirit of council and might, the spirit of knowledge and of the fear of the Lord." Isaiah 11:2 emphasis added.

When John wrote to the seven churches he mentioned the greeting of the "seven wisdoms." This greeting went this way: "John to the seven churches which are in Asia Grace be unto you and peace from him which is and which was and which is to come and from the seven spirits which are before his throne."

MOM WISDOM BIRTHED THE LORD JESUS.

"Now the birth of Jesus Christ was as follows: after his mother Mary was betrothed to Joseph, before they came together, she was found with child of the Holy Spirit." Matthew 1:18 Emphasis Added.

To confirm this to be true, Jesus made this statement: "But wisdom is justified of all her children."
Luke 7: 35 / Matthew 11:19 Emphasis Added.

The Earthly Strange Woman was shown in Zechariah chapter 5.

But the Heavenly Woman Wisdom, is revealed this way in Revelation 12:1-17. "Now a great sign appeared in heaven: a woman (Wisdom) clothed with the sun, with the moon (The Bride of Christ) under her feet, and on her head a garland of twelve stars. Then being with child, (The Lord Jesus Christ) she cried out in labor and pain to give birth.

And another sign appeared in heaven: behold a great, fiery red dragon (Lucifer, Satan) having seven heads and ten horns, and seven diadems on his heads. His tail drew a third of the stars of heaven (fallen angels) and threw them to the earth. And the dragon stood before the woman who was ready to give birth, to devour her Child as soon as it was born. (Matthew 2: 1- 18) She bore a male Child who was to rule all nations with a rod of iron. And her Child was caught up to God and his throne. (Acts 1: 9) And the woman fled into the wilderness, where she has a place prepared by God, that they should feed her there one thousand two hundred and sixty days. Emphasis Added.

Wisdom, (Mom Wisdom) is justified of all her children. The Amplified Bible puts it this way, saying: "Yet wisdom is vindicated (shown to be true and divine) by all her children [by their life, character, and deeds]." Luke 7:35 Amplified Bible with emphasis added.

My advise is to pray to the Heavenly Father that he would send Mom Wisdom to you and keep you from the strange Woman, For the Heavenly Father is still saying to us:
"Hearken unto me now therefore, O you children, and attend to the words of my mouth. Let not your heart decline to her ways, go not astray in her paths. For she has cast down many wounded: yea, many strong men have been slain by her. Her house is the way to hell, going down to the chambers of death. Proverbs   7:24-27,   emphasis   added.

17 GOD DOESN'T ANSWER MY PRAYERS

Why doesn't God answer my prayers?

Dear reader, I have no knowledge of my own. Here is what the Holy Bible has to say about this question.

James 4:1-3 Amplified Bible
What leads to strife (discord and feuds) and how do conflicts (quarrels and fighting's) originate among you? Do they not arise from your sensual desires that are ever warring in your bodily members? You are jealous and covet [what others have] and your desires go unfulfilled; [so] you become murderers. [To hate is to murder as far as your hearts are concerned.] You burn with envy and anger and are not able to obtain [the gratification, the contentment, and the happiness that you seek], so you fight and war. You do not have, because you do not ask. [Or] you do ask [God for them] and yet fail to receive, because you ask with wrong purpose and evil, selfish motives. Your intention is [when you get what you desire] to spend it in sensual pleasures.

1 John 5:14-15 Amplified Bible
And this is the confidence (the assurance, the privilege of boldness) which we have in Him: [we are sure] that if we ask anything (make any request) according to His will (in agreement with His own plan), He listens to and hears us. And if (since) we [positively] know that He listens to us in whatever we ask, we also know [with settled and absolute knowledge] that we have [granted us as our present possessions] the requests made of Him.

Proverbs 21:13 KJV
Whosoever continues to stop his ears at the cry of the poor, he also shall cry himself, but shall not be heard.

Proverbs 28:9 Amplified Bible
He who turns away his ear from hearing the law [of God and man], even his prayer is an abomination, hateful and revolting [to God].

Psalm 66:18-20 Amplified Bible
If I regard iniquity in my heart, the Lord will not hear me; But certainly God has heard me; He has given heed to the voice of my prayer. Blessed be God, Who has not rejected my prayer nor removed His mercy and loving-

kindness from being [as it always is] with me.

1 Peter 3:7 Amplified Bible
In the same way you married men should live considerately with [your wives], with an intelligent recognition [of the marriage relation], honoring the woman as [physically] the weaker, but [realizing that you] are joint heirs of the grace (God's unmerited favor) of life, in order that your prayers may not be hindered and cut off. [Otherwise you cannot pray effectively.]

Once the Lord was so through with his people for their many abominations, he said and recorded this in Jeremiah 15:1 AMPC
Then the Lord said to me (Jeremiah), Though Moses and Samuel stood [interceding for them] before Me, yet My mind could not be turned with favor toward this people [Judah]. Send them out of My sight and let them go!

Here God's people had sinned so much to where no one could pray to him to stop his judgment upon them.
Sometimes I believe that is the case with certain Nations or individuals alike, they themselves would have to talk to the Most High and persuade him of their true repentance.

Therefore, since we are justified
(acquitted, a declared righteous, and given a right standing with God) through faith, let us [grasp the fact that we] have [the peace of reconciliation to hold and to enjoy] peace with God through our Lord Jesus Christ (the Messiah, the Anointed One). Romans 5:1 Amplified Bible.

I hope these scriptures have brought you more clarity about that question. There are more answers in the Holy Bible, I do encourage you all to search the rest of the reasons why prayers are not heard, and don't just take my scripture   search   as   the   sum   total   of   all   things.

18 THE MEANING OF LIFE

What's the meaning of life? What does God want me to do?

Ecclesiastes 12:13-14 KJVS
Let us hear the conclusion of the whole matter: Fear God, and keep his commandments: for this is the whole duty of man. For God shall bring every work into judgment, with every secret thing, whether it be good, or whether it be evil.

Even though the Heavenly Father has set up his new will and testament; we all should still go back and see how he is concerning following his words through the Son Jesus to all of us alive today. For Moses said to our forefathers: "The Lord your God will raise up unto you a Prophet from the midst of you (Israel), of your brethren, like unto me, unto him you shall hearken; according to all that you desired of the Lord your God in Horeb in the day of the assembly, saying, let me not hear again the voice of the Lord my God, neither let me see this great fire any more, that I die not.

And the Lord said unto me, they have well-spoken that which they have spoken. I will raise them up a Prophet from among their brethren, like unto you, and will put my words in his mouth; and he shall speak unto them all that I shall command him. And it shall come to pass, that whosoever will not hearken unto my words which he shall speak in my name, I will require it of him. And again: For Moses truly said unto the fathers, A prophet shall the Lord your God raise up unto you of your brethren, like unto me; him shall you hear in all things whatsoever he shall say unto you. And it shall come to pass, that every soul, which will not hear that prophet, shall be destroyed from among the people. Deuteronomy 18:15 – 19 / Acts 3: 22, 23

This word has been passed down from the Godhead to Moses, then, from Moses to our fathers; Then, from our Heavenly Father again; (through Jesus the Messiah), to the obedient chosen Israelite Children of our fathers, (the Apostles), to all of us who are alive this day – (Judeans, Gentiles bond and free); basically all mankind. The prophesied Messiah: had this to say before he went back to the Heavenly Father: After finishing his work.

And Jesus said unto (his disciples) Go you into all the world, and preach the gospel to every creature. He that believes and is baptized shall be saved; but he that believes not shall be damned. Mark 16: 15,16 Emphasis Added.

What an amazing thing this is, (from old to new) it still stands, that we as modern day believers must take this all into account: that as it was then, so it is today: here is a summary / complete run down I put together to show us what all took place and what is now required for us to do this day.

The Israel of old was under a hard task master Pharaoh. (Exodus 1: 8- 14) Which represents Satan worldly rule Luke 4:5 ,6 emphasis added.

They were under bitter and hard bondage naturally, then of sin spiritually (Luke 13: 15, 17 / Acts 10:38 / 1 John 3:8. Next; God chose an Earthly type Messiah Moses. (Exodus 3:10) to free his people; then a Heavenly, once and for-all Messiah; Jesus the Anointed one. (Matthew 1: 20, 21 / John 8:31- 36 / Hebrews 10: 5- 9).

God then brought them out of the land of Egypt (Exodus 29:46 / Exodus 19:4 / Deuteronomy 4:20). Now likewise through his Son, he brought us out of the bondage of sin, from under a cruel task master Satan: (Hebrews 2:14,15 / Colossians 2:13-15). And while being made free; the Children of Israel were to receive and obey Gods law or word (Exodus 19:20-25; 20: 1- 19).

Seeing they requested Moses to translate for God and they said they would hear; God held them to it (Deuteronomy 4: 8-14, 33,36 / 5:2- 28), but they did not continue in it.

Then God scattered our fathers to all nations (Deuteronomy 4: 25- 31),

Now being in other Nations under the whole earth, he came up with this plan as it is written: I (Paul) ask then: Has God totally rejected and disowned His people? Of course not! Why, I myself am an Israelite, a descendant of Abraham, a member of the tribe of Benjamin! No, God has not rejected and disowned His people [whose destiny] He had marked out and appointed and foreknown from the beginning. Do you not know what the Scripture says of Elijah, how he pleads with God against Israel? Lord, they have killed Your prophets; they have demolished Your altars, and I alone am left, and they seek my life.

But what is God's reply to him? I have kept for Myself seven thousand men who have not bowed the knee to Baal! So too at the present time there is a remnant (a small believing minority), selected (chosen) by grace (by God's unmerited favor and graciousness). But if it is by grace (His unmerited favor and graciousness), it is no longer conditioned on works or anything men have done. Otherwise, grace would no longer be grace [it would be meaningless]. What then [shall we conclude]? Israel failed to obtain what it sought [God's favor by obedience to the Law]. Only the elect (those chosen few) obtained it, while the rest of them became callously indifferent (blinded, hardened, and made insensible to it). As it is written, God gave them a spirit (an attitude) of stupor, eyes that should not see and ears that should not hear, [that has continued] down to this very day.

And David says, Let their table (their feasting, banqueting) become a snare and a trap, a pitfall and a just retribution [rebounding like a boomerang upon them]; Let their eyes be darkened (dimmed) so that they cannot see, and make them bend their back [stooping beneath their burden] forever. So I ask, Have they stumbled so as to fall [to their utter spiritual ruin, irretrievably]? By no means! But through their false step and transgression salvation [has come] to the Gentiles, so as to arouse Israel [to see and feel what they forfeited] and so to make them jealous. Now if their stumbling (their lapse, their transgression) has so enriched the world [at large], and if [Israel's] failure means such riches for the Gentiles, think what an enrichment and greater advantage will follow their full reinstatement! But now I am speaking to you who are Gentiles.

Inasmuch then as I (Paul) am an apostle to the Gentiles, I lay great stress on my ministry and magnify my office, In the hope of making my fellow Jews jealous [in order to stir them up to imitate, copy, and appropriate], and thus managing to save some of them. For if their rejection and exclusion from the benefits of salvation were [overruled] for the reconciliation of a world to God, what will their acceptance and admission mean? [It will be nothing short of] life from the dead! Now if the first handful of dough offered as the first fruits [Abraham and the patriarchs] is consecrated (holy), so is the whole mass [the nation of Israel]; and if the root [Abraham] is consecrated (holy), so are the branches. But if some of the branches were broken off, while you, a wild olive shoot, were grafted in among them to share the richness [of the root and sap] of the olive tree, do not boast over the branches and pride yourself at their expense.

If you do boast and feel superior, remember it is not you that support the root, but the root [that supports] you. You will say then, Branches were broken (pruned) off so that I might be grafted in! That is true. But they were broken (pruned) off because of their unbelief (their lack of real faith), and you are established through faith [because you do believe]. So do not become proud and conceited, but rather stand in awe and be reverently afraid. For if God did not spare the natural branches [because of unbelief], neither will He spare you [if you are guilty of the same offense]. Then note and appreciate the gracious kindness and the severity of God: severity toward those who have fallen, but God's gracious kindness to you — provided you continue in His grace and abide in His kindness; otherwise you too will be cut off (pruned away). And even those others [the fallen branches, Jews], if they do not persist in [clinging to] their unbelief, will be grafted in, for God has the power to graft them in again.

For if you have been cut from what is by nature a wild olive tree, and against nature grafted into a cultivated olive tree, how much easier will it be to graft these natural [branches] back on [the original parent stock of] their own olive tree. Lest you be self-opinionated (wise in your own conceits), I do not want you to miss this hidden truth and mystery, brethren: a hardening (insensibility) has [temporarily] befallen a part of Israel [to last] until the full number of the ingathering of the Gentiles has come in, And so all Israel will be saved. As it is written, The Deliverer will come from Zion, He will banish ungodliness from Jacob.

And this will be My covenant (My agreement) with them when I shall take away their sins. From the point of view of the Gospel (good news), they [the Jews, at present] are enemies [of God], which is for your advantage and benefit. But from the point of view of God's choice (of election, of divine selection), they are still the beloved (dear to Him) for the sake of their forefathers. For God's gifts and His call are irrevocable. [He never withdraws them when once they are given, and He does not change His mind about those to whom He gives His grace or to whom He sends His call.] Just as you were once disobedient and rebellious toward God but now have obtained [His] mercy, through their disobedience, So they also now are being disobedient [when you are receiving mercy], that they in turn may one day, through the mercy you are enjoying, also receive mercy [that they may share the mercy which has been shown to you-through you as messengers of the Gospel to them].

For God has consigned (penned up) all men to disobedience, only that He may have mercy on them all [alike]. Oh, the depth of the riches and wisdom and knowledge of God! How unfathomable (inscrutable, unsearchable) are His judgments (His decisions)! And how untraceable (mysterious, undiscoverable) are His ways (His methods, His paths)! For who has known the mind of the Lord and who has understood His thoughts, or who has [ever] been His counselor? Or who has first given God anything that he might be paid back or that he could claim a recompense? For from Him and through Him and to Him are all things. [For all things originate with Him and come from Him; all things live through Him, and all things center in and tend to consummate and to end in Him.] To Him be glory forever! Amen (so be it).

I hope this book has blessed you the reader. I hope the things mentioned was understandable. The Holy Bible speaks for itself, there are many answers in it, if we just search it out. Though many will not believe it's God inspired, it really doesn't matter, it still stands true. I'm just greatful to our God for allowing it to get to us in this millennium.

Though many have added or taken away from it, it's yet amazing how they simply can't kill it. Even if they take it away physically by a law, they yet can't take it out of our hearts. This concludes my Book "Understanding and knowing God through some of life's hard questions"

Get to know the Creator of Heaven and Earth for yourselves, don't just take my perspective on things, have your own, just as long as it lines up with scripture and doesn't mislead the new seeker. Finally get to know for yourself what this statement means,

"I am the LORD which exercise loving-kindness, judgment, and righteousness, in the earth: for in these things I delight, say the LORD."

THE END

ABOUT THE AUTHOR

I'm a 48 year young Happily Married Man - I have 3 young adults of my own and 1 Grandchild - I'm definitely a God fearing - Born again scribe disciple of the Lord and Savior Yahweh and his Holy Child Jesus (Yeshua) the Christ - This blook came about when I received a warning to prepare and get busy / ready to fulfill my earthly destiny - started writing to record a specific experience or journey I had coming up in the Christian faith. After falling down and reverting instead of converting - I was lovingly dealt with by the Heavenly Father - who's been so patient with me. My motivation to come out of hiding was geared on my heart to help others - this is my gift to you - we're gonna make it - I don't know who all I will help but - the Lord did give me a vision of a lot of people thanking me for what I did in life to help them. I can never forget it and decided to embrace my call in life and share my testimony. We all have one and it's by that we will overcome this world.

This is his first Book he ever produced. He didn't plan on putting this out to the public, but felt divinely inspired to release it to whomsoever will. Christopher became a believer in 1995 and has an unusual story to tell about his process of leaving a worldly nature to a spiritual nature. He has had his share of confrontations both naturally and spiritually, and feels he has something to share with the entire World if given the chance. He believes that we all need one another as believers to overcome the "Darkness on the horizon," and hope to God that - his body of believers can truly come to a unity in and of the faith in which they stand.

Thank you for your interest in my book - Do check out my other book titled: "What Did Jesus Say To do?"
this book was made and written for my own personal use- to have something

to survive and meditate on in these dark days. Seeing I'm not selfish - I decided to share what I know having little or no money with an average education.

Please forgive me for the poorly edited manuscript. - What you are seeing and hearing was my very first manuscript ever - I'm Hoping to perfect the manuscript one day. There have been (and still are) many Spiritual battles I faced in order to get this out to the public. - I'm Hoping to help - if but one person in the whole wide world - but I'm willing to settle for many - My souls purpose of producing this book was for daily meditation.

God bless and keep you all.

Respectfully

Christopher